THE ULTIMATE

Missionary

COMPANION

AUDIO PRODUCTS BY ED J. PINEGAR:

After Your Mission

Being a Missionary

Especially for Missionaries, vol. 1-6

Hope in Christ

Man Is That He Might Have Joy

Overcoming Twelve Tough Temptations

Pleasing God

Power Tools for Missionaries, vol. 1-4

Preparing for a Mission

Turn it Over to the Lord

Preparing the Lord's Missionary

THE ULTIMATE

Missionary

COMPANION

ED *J.* PINEGAR

Covenant Communications, Inc.

Covenant®

Cover photo by Maren Ogden

Cover design copyrighted 2001 by Covenant Communications, Inc.

Published by Covenant Communications, Inc.
American Fork, Utah

Printed in the United States of America
First Printing: June 2001

08 07 06 05   10 9 8 7 6 5

ISBN 1-57734-830-3   3296   6565   4/06

DEDICATION

This book is dedicated to all the wonderful missionaries throughout the world—both past and present, young and old. I'm especially grateful to the missionaries of the MTC, and the England London South Mission that I have had the privilege of serving with. Surely the Lord is pleased with all their righteous efforts.

ACKNOWLEDGMENTS

I express my gratitude to Covenant Communications, with a special thanks to Shauna Nelson and Angela Colvin, who have made the editorial changes that have enhanced the quality of the book. I would also like to sincerely thank Grant V. Harrison for some wonderful information in chapter ten, and Nola Delange for her generous help in typing this manuscript.

I also express gratitude to my sweetheart who has been my companion as we have served together in this glorious work.

PREFACE

As missionaries, we realize that the source of all our success is in the strength of the Lord (see Alma 26:11–12). The Lord goes before us and helps us in all things (see D&C 84:85–88). The Spirit provides the words we need to say at the very moment (see D&C 100:5–6). Our converts are converted by that same Spirit. With the Lord, the Spirit, and our mortal companions, we can bring souls unto Christ. This is our joy and our glory (see D&C 18:10–16; Alma 29:9–10).

This book is simply a resource to help you truly be a mighty instrument in the hands of the Lord. You must always remember that the ultimate missionary companion is the Spirit. As you study and obtain the word, and make yourselves worthy of the Spirit's companionship, you can truly be a light unto the world and the saviors of mankind (see D&C 103:9–10).

Ed J. Pinegar

⁕ TABLE OF CONTENTS ⁕

$\mathscr{C}$HAPTER 1

THE PURPOSE AND JOY OF MISSIONARY WORK

In August of 1975 President Benson gave a marvelous talk at the Tokyo, Japan Area Conference. In that talk he quoted President Spencer W. Kimball on the need to enhance our vision of missionary work: "We must raise our sights, and get a vision of the magnitude and urgency of this great missionary work" ("Safety in the Face of Wickedness," Conference Report, 8–10). The Church in this dispensation is to proclaim the gospel, to perfect the Saints, and redeem the dead. Why is this so important? Everything that the Church, which is the kingdom of God, does here upon the earth is for one purpose, and that is to assist in Heavenly Father's work. "For behold, this is my work and my glory—to bring to pass the immortality and eternal life of man" (Moses 1:39). That means everyone. Everything Heavenly Father does, and will do, is so that you and I can be happy and return to His presence forever.

The worth of souls is great in the sight of God. How great shall be your joy with those people whom you help come unto Christ. And if your joy be great with one, think how great it will be with many (see D&C 18:10–16). In other words, Heavenly Father's priority is His children. Now I don't know what that does for you, but that gives me eternal self-esteem because I, Ed Jolley Pinegar, am Heavenly Father's son, and you are His sons and daughters. And the greatest thing you'll ever do on this earth is to help one of His children return home.

"Seek ye first the kingdom of God, and his righteousness; and all these things shall be added unto you" (Matt. 6:33). In the Joseph Smith translation of the Bible that verse now reads, "Seek ye first to build up the kingdom of God, and to establish his righteousness; and all these things shall be added unto you" (JS—M 6:38). Build up the kingdom! What is the kingdom made of? Men and women. You and me. When you bless someone's life, you elevate your own life. When you've "done it unto one of the least of these my brethren," the Savior said, you've "done it unto me" (Matt. 25:40). We must catch the vision of the worth of souls. Once you understand the worth of a soul, you'll want to share the gospel of Jesus Christ. You'll want to help other people be happy because it's the only way you'll ever be happy on this earth and in the hereafter. If you don't seek to serve, and seek to bless, it's very difficult to grow.

The sons of Mosiah and Alma were not only inactive in the Church, but were engaged in active persecution. Alma the Younger was the ringleader. However, they all repented of their sins, became totally converted, and became great and wonderful missionaries. I love Alma, Ammon, Omner, Himni, and Aaron. Did they have the vision of missionary work? Did they care about other people's souls?

> Now they [the sons of Mosiah] were desirous that salvation should be declared to every creature, for they could not bear that any human soul should perish; yea, even the very thoughts that any soul should endure endless torment did cause them to quake and tremble (Mosiah 28:3).

Do you feel that way? Do you quake and tremble if you see someone doing something wrong? Would you hurry and say a prayer if somebody was struggling and not coming to church, and say, "Heavenly Father, bless Billy, or Bobby, or Sally, or Suzy, and please help them catch the vision; bless their lives," instead of saying, "they deserve what they get." You'll always know how Christlike you are by how much concern you have for others. For that is the barometer of your love and Christlike capacity.

The sons of Mosiah had great concern for their fellowmen. They knew the worth of souls. They had the vision in their mind. Alma the Younger felt likewise:

> I know that which the Lord hath commanded me, and I glory in it. I do not glory of myself, but I glory in that which the

Lord hath commanded me; yea, and this is my glory, that perhaps I may be an instrument in the hands of God to bring some soul to repentance; and this is my joy (Alma 29:9).

Now he didn't say, "when I graduate from college with a 4.0, then I'll feel good. When I'm the captain of the football team or do a slam dunk, then I'll be ok." He said, "if I can just be an instrument in the hands of the Lord, this is my glory and my joy."

He goes on to say in verse 10:

And behold, when I see many of my brethren truly penitent [or repentant], and coming to the Lord their God, then is my soul filled with joy; then do I remember what the Lord has done for me, yea, even that he hath heard my prayer; yea, then do I remember his merciful arm which he extended towards me (Alma 29:10).

The joy of helping people repent—that's the vision. Why do you think all the missionaries come home and say the same thing at the pulpit? "It was the happiest eighteen months of my life. It was the greatest two years of my life." I mean, do you like getting up at 6:30 AM and working twelve hours a day, every day for eighteen to twenty-four months, not watching any movies or TV? Hooray, hooray, hooray! No TV, hooray, hooray, hooray! Great missionaries have the vision—that's why they work so hard.

One time I was talking with an elderly gentlemen who was about seventy-five or eighty years old. He related this conversation with Elder Haight. He said, "Well, Elder Haight, I'm so old I might die on my mission." Elder Haight said, "What a great place to die." Think about it. There could be no better thing to do or place to be, than serving your God and your fellowmen.

Now, are you catching the vision? The vision of the work and the vision of yourself in regards to the work? The Whitmer brothers, John and Peter, came to see the Prophet Joseph, wondering what would be the most important thing they could do. Joseph received Doctrine and Covenants 15 and 16 in response. They are almost identical: "And now behold I say unto you," Brother Whitmer, or to you or to me; remember, we put our names in the place of the individual named in the scripture.

> And now, behold, I say unto you [Elders and Sisters], that
> the thing which will be of the most worth unto you will be to
> declare repentance unto this people, that you may bring souls
> unto me, that you may rest with them in the kingdom of my
> Father. Amen.(D&C16:6).

That is the greatest thing you can ever do.

We have eight children in our family. Sister Pinegar and I were blessed with a large family, and I want you to know all of them came on this earth as investigators. We taught all eight of them, and all eight were baptized. Therefore, we have eight converts in our family. Everywhere you go you are teaching the gospel by principle, by precept, and by example. That's the vision. This earth was made only to accommodate the vision of saving souls; and that's why you, the noble and great, were preserved to come forth at this time, to do all these wonderful things.

On October 3, 1918, the Prophet Joseph F. Smith received section 138 of the Doctrine and Covenants.

> I observed that they were also among the noble and great
> ones who were chosen in the beginning to be rulers in the
> Church of God. Even before they [or you] were born, they, with
> many others, received their first lessons in the world of spirits
> and were prepared to come forth in the due time of the Lord to
> labor in his vineyard for the salvation of the souls of men (D&C
> 138:55–56).

I hope you understand the vision of the work, and that you are starting to understand the vision of your responsibility in building up the kingdom of God. When you were baptized you covenanted to be willing "to stand as witnesses of God at all times and in all things, and in all places" (Mosiah 18:9). To stand as a witness for God always. The young women of the Church know this as part of their theme, which they say every week. What do witnesses do? We testify. What do we testify of? That God is our Father, Jesus is the Christ, the Book of Mormon is true, Joseph Smith is a prophet, the gospel has been restored, the true Church is on the earth today, and we are led by a living prophet. We are witnesses. We testify. That's our duty and our joy.

"For they [you and me] were set to be a light unto the world"
(D&C 103:9). The light of the world is the Lord Jesus Christ. The light
that we possess is the amount of light of the Lord Jesus Christ we have
within us. So you are sent to be a light unto the world. But that's only
part of it. The rest of the verse reads, "And to be the saviors of men; And
inasmuch as they are not the saviors of men" (in other words, if you're
not out there with your light, helping people come unto Christ this is
what happens), "they [you and I] are as salt that has lost its savor"
(v. 10), or become impure or has no value.

If you, as the salt of the earth, don't hold up this light, you've lost
your savor. "And [are] thenceforth good for nothing but to be cast out
and trodden under foot of men" (v. 10). Life is serious business. Our
business on this earth is to help Heavenly Father build His kingdom
by blessing our brothers and sisters, and that's it. That's what we're
here for.

When I was president of the MTC, I remember watching all
the missionaries coming in, and I'd just almost want to cry
because I'd see them as the Lord's anointed. They would prepare,
and they would go out and serve with all their heart, might, mind,
and soul. "And ye shall go forth in the power of my Spirit,
preaching my gospel, two by two, in my name, lifting up your
voices as with the sound of a trump, declaring my word like unto
angels of God" (D&C 42:6). That is wonderful. You go out like
angels of God. Do you know what ministering angels do?
Ministering angels call people to repentance.

Missionaries are to preach the gospel of Jesus Christ and help
people to have faith unto repentance that they might be saved. That's
what missionaries do.

THE LORD WILL HELP YOU

"Treasure up in your minds continually the words of life, and it
shall be given you in the very hour that portion that shall be meted
unto every man" (D&C 84:85). "For it shall be given you in the very
hour, yea, in the very moment, what ye shall say" (D&C 100:6). The
Lord is with you when you are a missionary (see D&C 84:86–88).
The key for all this to happen, as missionaries, is to have the Spirit.

For without the Spirit, you cannot preach, you cannot teach, you cannot understand, and you cannot be lead. The Spirit is the key. And with the Spirit you can do all things because the Spirit will direct you. It is the Spirit that will convert.

Let me illustrate these points with an experience I had some years ago. It was about 1969 when a young girl named Susan Gerszewski came to see me. "Bishop you've got to take my name off the records of the Church."

I said, "Oh Susan, what's wrong?"

"My brothers think I'm a dork for being here at BYU, and I can't stand the pressure when I go home and my parents are wondering what's gone wrong with me."

And then all of a sudden, the Lord stepped in and words came out of my mouth like this: "Susan, I promise you that if you stay faithful, your brothers will join the Church and your parents' hearts will soften." Now how could I say that? I couldn't. Only the Lord could.

She said, " Oh I just don't know Bishop, I just don't know." I said, "Well Susan, is the Book of Mormon true?"

"Well, of course it is Bishop."

"Do you love the Savior and do you believe in Heavenly Father?"

"Yes I do."

"Is the Prophet the head of the Church today?"

"Of course."

"Is this the true Church?"

"Of course it is. But I just can't stand the pressure."

I said, "Susan, will you be willing to try, because the Lord just gave you a promise."

She said, "Well I guess I can try." That year she moved out of the ward and I lost track of her.

Well, at BYU in 1972 I volunteered to teach another religion class, besides the Book of Mormon, before going to my dental office. It was the Gospel Principles and Practices class. There were about sixty students in the class, and life was going just merrily along, and on the last day to drop the class, this student came up to me and he said, "I've got to drop your class."

I asked, "How come?"

He said, "Well I'm on scholarship, and if I don't get a B or a B+ I could lose my scholarship; and I got a C+ on the test, and besides I'm not a Mormon."

I looked at his little information sheet I had him fill out before class, and I'd missed it. He'd checked "nonmember" so close to the "member" that I'd missed it.

I said, "Well Jim, you mean you're just afraid you won't get a B?"

He said, "Well, how can I? I'm not a member and I just can't risk it."

I said, "Jim I've got an idea. Do you normally study once a week for this class?"

He answered, "Yes."

I said, "Jim, I've got it. Would you mind studying with me Tuesday nights before class on Wednesday, for an hour?"

He said, "Yes, but what will that do?"

I continued, "Well Jim, you want a B, right? Do you know who makes out the grade?"

He answered, "Well, you do."

I smiled. "That's right Jim, I'm guaranteeing you a B or a B+."

"You mean you'll guaran . . ."

"I guarantee it. Look, I'm going to teach you extra Tuesday nights. If you're in my house for an hour, well, I'll make up the test too. I'll even help you prepare for the test. Jim, I'm guaranteeing you this."

Jim said, "Well that's a deal, I'm going to study with you." So Jim came up to my house, and this went on for a couple of weeks, and then one day he asked, "Hey Brother Ed, could I bring my brother and my roommate up? I mean, we have banana splits and root beer floats and doughnuts every study night; we might as well have parties when you teach."

And so I said, "You bet, you bring them up." So we went along for four more weeks, and then this one night they came up and they were kind of kidding around a lot, so I said, "You guys are sure having a hoot tonight. What's up around here?"

They looked at each other as if to say, "OK, who's going to tell him," and then Jim finally said, "Brother Ed, we've been thinking, and we talked to our bishop, and we all want to be baptized, and will you baptize us and confirm us members of the Church next week?"

As I floated down from the ceiling I said, "Yes Jim. I will, I will, I will." Well, his name was Jim Gerszewski, but I had mispronounced his name. Jim was Susan's brother; Susan was at the baptism, and joy was felt by all.

Now you tell me that God our Father and Jesus Christ are not in charge of everything on this earth. How could those words come out of my mouth, "Your brothers will join the Church"? How, two years later, could one of those brothers be in my class? There were 20,000 students at BYU. Don't tell me that the Lord's hand isn't in all things that are good. All three boys served missions. All three were married in the temple.

So as I learned again that year, the Spirit "will show unto you all things what ye should do" (2 Ne. 32:5). Why is this so important? Because the vision in missionary work is that you must prepare people to feel the Spirit; and their needs are individual—you've got to be in tune to what they need. Then, once they feel the Spirit, you can invite them to make a commitment. Once you've invited them to make a commitment, you must follow up with them to help them keep that commitment.

This is the best way to help people stay committed. It shows our love, and in the vision of the work, that's what we do. We show love. Teach by the Spirit, and people will want to make a change in their lives. We've all had the Spirit in our lives, and sometimes we don't recognize it and give credit to our Heavenly Father. In Doctrine and Covenants 11 we read, "Verily, verily, I say unto thee, put your trust in that Spirit which leadeth to do good." Have you ever had a desire to do good? Of course. That's the Spirit. "To do justly." Have you ever been honest in your dealings and just with your fellowmen? Of course. That's the Spirit. "To walk humbly." Have you ever been humbled? Of course you have. That's the Spirit. Have you ever made a righteous judgment? Of course you have. And of these the Lord says, "and this is my Spirit" (D&C 11:12).

"Verily, verily, I say unto you, I will impart unto you of my Spirit, which shall enlighten your mind, which shall fill your soul with joy" (D&C 11:13). Every time a missionary preaches or teaches, every time you feel a good feeling, it is the Spirit. The Spirit is what makes missionary work successful. For without the Spirit, there is no conversion. So, the vision of the work is that we understand the power of the Spirit. You teach with that Spirit. You teach with that power to such a point that you have a power to convince men and women to come unto Christ because they feel that Spirit and act upon those feelings. You have the vision. You realize it's the Spirit that counts.

CONCLUSION

It is by the power of the Spirit that people are committed to the gospel. This is the purpose of missionary work—to invite all to come unto Christ and be perfected in Him (see Moroni 10:32).

⇥ 𝒞HAPTER 2 ⇤

PREPARING FOR A MISSION

So, now that we know we need the vision to succeed, how do we get it? Are we willing to prepare? So many people want to win, but as Coach Lavell Edwards says, "Maybe they don't want to prepare to win." Preparation precedes the power to become a pure disciple of Christ. The following principles will help you prepare for this most important battle.

THE VISION AND DESIRE

Now, if we have this vision and understand and appreciate it, then we begin to have a desire. We want to be missionaries. We want to share the gospel. We want to prepare. We want to be an instrument in the hands of the Lord. This desire, when it swells up within us, will cause us to work harder. When Alma the Younger was converted he was like the sons of Mosiah; they couldn't wait to go on their mission. When Enos was converted he prayed all day and into the night and his sins were forgiven, his guilt was swept away, and he was truly converted. He began to pray for the Nephites, and he prayed for the Lamanites, and then he implored Heavenly Father to save the record, because he wanted everyone to hear the record because it was so good and so precious. You see what happens? Our desire begins to increase when our conversion to Christ is real. We want to be missionaries for the Lord. That's what desire can do for us, because when we have a clear vision, we have a desire, and then we become worthy disciples of Jesus Christ.

WORTHINESS

Missionaries teach faith unto repentance. In all the discussions, you first preach faith to accept the doctrine, then repentance to change people's lives and help them live the doctrine. You can't preach faith unto repentance until you live faith unto repentance. So your first step in preparing to become a good missionary is to repent, to make sure that you are worthy instruments in the hands of the Lord. Because if we're not worthy, we can't have the Spirit. If we don't have the Spirit, we can't teach, we can't preach, we can't be led, we can't be directed, we can't know the things to say—we simply can't do anything. When conversion happens, it happens because the people's hearts are softened, and then they feel the Spirit, and then they're invited to make and keep commitments and they change.

It's interesting when people write and explain the reasons they joined the Church: "I felt their love so much, I had to listen to what they said"; or, "While listening I felt the Spirit and I knew I had to be baptized." So as missionaries, you and I must be worthy instruments by practicing faith unto repentance, being full of charity, and being exactly and courageously obedient so we can enjoy the Spirit.

We must be worthy to go to the temple, the house of the Lord. We must believe in God as our Father, in Jesus as the Christ, and in the Holy Ghost. We must have a testimony that Jesus atoned for our sins, and that through Him all mankind might be saved. We must sustain our prophets, seers, and revelators. We must be honest in all our dealings. We must be pure in all ways: morally, intellectually, and spiritually. We must keep the Word of Wisdom. We must pay our tithing. We must make sure our family dynamics are in harmony with the teachings of the Church. We must be totally, completely repentant. And if we do these things, we will be a clean, prepared instrument in the hands of the Lord.

Earlier in my life I was a practicing dentist. I would go to the hospital and do oral surgery to remove the third molars (wisdom teeth). I can still remember preparing for surgery with the nurses around, the anesthesiologists in the operating room, and everything ready to go for the operation. Then I would say, "scalpel," and the scalpel was in my hand. I would retract the cheek a little bit and make an incision, lay back the tissue, and then I would start to remove the impacted third molar. Those instruments did whatever I wanted them to do because I had them in my hand and I was in control. I knew what I was supposed to do and so I was hopefully very kind and efficient. Well you know what? The instrument was clean, it was pure, it was sharp. Each instrument had a purpose to perform in my hand, for I was the doctor. And that's what our relationship is with our Savior. He is our master, and we are instruments in His hands—submissive to His will, provided we are clean and pure and know our purpose.

CHARITY

Now, as we become worthy, clean, and pure, we will start to prepare by doing specific things to be better instruments in the hands of the Lord. Preparation begins today and goes on forever because we want to be just like the Lord Jesus Christ. The Lord said, "What manner of men ought ye to be? Verily I say unto you, even as I am" (3 Ne. 27:27). We are to be like Christ. He said, "Therefore I would that ye should be perfect even as I, or your Father who is in heaven is perfect" (3 Ne. 12:48). So the Lord expects us to start to be Christlike. In fact, He expects us to be full of charity. Remember why people are baptized? They feel your love, and are compelled to listen to what you say. Well, when we have the pure love of Christ within us we will be like Jesus Christ. We will have His love. We will radiate His countenance. We will hold up His light. "Therefore, hold up your light that it may shine unto the world. Behold I am the light which ye shall hold up—that which ye have seen me do" (3 Ne. 18:24). So when we radiate His goodness and His light, we radiate Jesus Christ. We have His image in our countenance. Have you received His image in your countenance? Have you had this mighty change of heart (see Alma 5:14)? Acquiring the attributes of Jesus Christ is part of the preparation. Doctrine and Covenants 4 is the missionary scripture. It is the standard and expectation missionaries should live by. "Remember faith, virtue, knowledge, temperance, patience, brotherly kindness, godliness, charity" (D&C 4:6). How? By being humble and diligent. If we are humble and diligent we will be dependent upon the Lord; and we'll work with all our heart, might, mind, and soul, to acquire these attributes of Christ, especially charity. When we have charity we possess many of the inner qualities we need to become a good missionary—the kind of missionary with whom the Lord is pleased. The kind who can be an ambassador and a disciple of Jesus Christ to preach His word to all the world.

GOSPEL KNOWLEDGE

We need gospel knowledge. We need to understand the word of the Lord. "The words of Christ will tell you all things what ye should do" (2 Ne. 32:3). If we hold to the iron rod, the mists of darkness or temptation will never take us away from the strait and narrow path (see 1 Ne. 15:24). Once we hold to the word of God, and begin to gain gospel knowledge, we will be strengthened. We will go to the tree of life whose fruit (the love of God—the Atonement of Jesus Christ) is desirable above all other things to make us happy. In other words, when we gain gospel knowledge to the point that we understand and appreciate it, our behaviors and attitudes will change, and we'll be happy because we have partaken of the goodness of God. We will be the most dynamic missionaries the Lord could have because we're prepared, because we have gospel knowledge. We will nurture the word with faith, diligence, and patience so it can grow to be a fruitful tree (see Alma 32:40–43).

TESTIMONY

As we gain this knowledge our testimonies will grow. We'll be able to stand up and say, "I testify that God our Father lives, Jesus is the Christ, the gospel has been restored, Joseph Smith was a prophet and we're led by a Prophet today, and the Book of Mormon is true," and we'll testify of this by the Spirit. We can do that as gospel knowledge becomes part of us. As we study and as we pray, our testimony will grow and we'll know we are about our Heavenly Father's work.

PRAYER

Prayer is a form of worship (see Alma 33:3). We have been commanded to call upon our Heavenly Father, for the benefits of prayer are all-encompassing in our lives. We must pray for strength (see Moses 1:20), to overcome temptation (see Alma 13:28), for others (see Mosiah 27:14), for humility and faith (see Hel. 3:35), and for the Spirit in our teaching (see D&C 42:14).

The blessings of prayer are clear for missionaries. We must pray always. We must go with a prayer in our hearts (see 3 Ne. 20:1). We should pray for those who know not God (Alma 6:6). We should pray for our investigators to know the truth by the power of the Spirit. We've been commanded to pray for all things (see Alma 34:17–28). We must pray as if everything depends upon the Lord, and then work as if everything depends upon us.

OBEDIENCE—THE FIRST LAW OF HEAVEN

In the mission field there's a great law—it's called obedience. In our mission it was called immediate, exact, and courageous obedience. Obedience is built upon love, faith, and trust in God. When we live the principle of obedience, we will be more diligent in being immediately, exactly, and courageously obedient.

A story is told of a young boy who wanted to fly a kite. He and his father purchased a kite along with two spools of string, which they put on one big spool. They fixed it all up and went out to fly their kite. The kite started taking off. "Dad, look at it go, look at it go!" Soon the kite soared higher and higher. They let all the string out. The boy pulled the string and said, "Dad, the string is holding it down. Look how tight it is. It's really tight. Let's cut it so the kite can fly up higher."

The dad said, "No, you don't understand, son. This is the law that holds the kite up. It needs the string."

The boy said, "Dad, look!" and he pulled on the string. "See, it's holding, it's tight, it's holding it down."

The father said, "No son, the string helps the kite fly."

"No it doesn't," insisted the boy.

"So you want to cut the string?" asked the dad.

"Yes, I want to let it fly up all the way, all the way to the clouds," replied the boy.

The dad said, "OK," and he took out his pocket knife and let the boy cut the string. Well, you know what happened next, the kite came crashing down to the ground. The boy looked at his dad and asked "why?"

To which the father replied, "Son, the string was part of the law by which the kite could fly." A lesson was learned about obedience to law. Everything is based upon a law.

> And if a person gains more knowledge and intelligence in this life through his diligence and obedience than another, he will have so much the advantage in the world to come. There is a law, irrevocably decreed in heaven before the foundations of this world, upon which all blessings are predicated—and when we obtain any blessing from God, it is by obedience to that law upon which it is predicated (D&C 130:19–21).

We get the blessing upon which the law is based. If we eat properly, we feel good. If we study, we learn. If we obey, we become free. Now, do you know what you get when you're obedient? When you are obedient you receive the greatest gift in all the world—the gift of the Spirit.

Every Sunday you go to church and you partake of the sacrament, and at the end of the sacramental prayer it says, "if ye keep my commandments," or in other words, if you are obedient, "ye shall have my Spirit to be with you." The Spirit will guide you, it will testify for you, it will lead you, it will correct you, it will comfort you, and it will show you all things what you should do (see 2 Ne. 32:5). You cannot do anything in the mission field without having the Spirit, and you can't have the Spirit unless you choose to be obedient. This is the hardest thing for missionaries to understand. If we are exactly, immediately, and courageously obedient in all things, the Lord will bless us. This is the test of life to see if we will obey (see Abr. 3:25). When obedience becomes your quest you will be happy and you will grow, and you will enjoy your mission. 1 Samuel 15:18–22 teaches that sacrifice is good, but that obedience is greater than sacrifice, because if we obey, we will always sacrifice. Obedience is the great law.

THE SPIRIT

When we become obedient we become Spirit-directed in all things. We will be led by the Spirit not knowing beforehand the things what we should do (see 1 Ne. 4:6). We can have the Spirit all day long and every day. The question is, are we worthy? When we feel a desire to do good, we have the Spirit. We will search the scriptures, say our prayers, and be kind to our fellowmen. The Spirit will show us and help us do all the things we should do. Sometimes we feel, "I'm not ready, I don't know how to do this, how can I ever do it?" The Lord and the Spirit will assist you. "I will go before your face. I will be on your right hand and on your left, and my Spirit shall be in your hearts, and mine angels round about you, to bear you up" (D&C 84:88). The Lord is there helping every missionary, every day, by the power of the Spirit. We give the credit to the Lord for all things. All good is from God. We get to be an instrument for the Lord and a conduit for the Spirit. Every week or so I get letters from missionaries. They say, "Oh Brother Ed it's just like you said, it's so great, I feel the Spirit and I'm so happy. We just baptized. The Lord is so good to us in our trials as well as our successes."

WORK

When we become Spirit-directed in all things, we will be willing to work with faith, diligence and patience. Faith has three degrees: (1) hope and belief, (2) the moving cause of all action, and (3) power to do all things. When faith is a part of us, we will be diligent, which means we work with all our heart, might, mind, and soul.

> One of the greatest secrets of missionary work is work! If missionaries work we will get the Spirit; if we get the Spirit, we will teach by the Spirit; and if we teach by the Spirit, we will touch the hearts of the people and we will be happy. There will be no homesickness, no worrying about families, for all time and talents and interests are centered on the work of the ministry. That's the secret—work, work, work. There is no satisfactory substitute, especially in missionary work (Ezra Taft Benson, in a mission presidents' seminar, Aug. 1982).

To prepare to be missionaries, we need to know how to work. Missionaries who took extra time and effort to do well in school or a job had usually learned how to work. They were always that much better as a missionary. Those who knew how to work were successful. Otherwise, I had to teach them how to work. I would tell them the story about how I was raised on a farm, and on our farm you had to work or you got spanked, and I learned right off that you worked or you perished. In the mission field, all the missionaries knew that President Pinegar loved them, but if they didn't want to work, I was very sad and I would call them in and say, "I don't feel so good. I don't know if you're working as hard as the Lord would want you to work." We would discuss the Atonement . Their gratitude would increase and they would start to cry, then I'd start to cry, and we'd cry together, and we'd agree that we would work harder, because there is nothing more joyous than working for the Lord. Think what the Savior and all the prophets have done for us. Appreciate what they did. Can you imagine what they went through? The price is high but it's worth it. Remember, learn to work. Get a job and organize your time wisely.

We need to have a plan; we need to organize our time. Missionaries who are prepared with every needful thing will reap the blessings of the Lord in all things. When you have a hard day, you get up and do it again, and you never quit, you never give up, you never give in, you never give out. You are always just working, doing the Lord's work. Learn that now and you'll be a better missionary.

SKILLS

With this preparation we will want to gain some skills, skills like being able to talk to people, being socially graceful—carrying on a conversation and turning it into a missionary opportunity. We can talk to people. We can learn to open our mouths. Remember what the Spirit will do, it will give us the very words we need to say at the very moment we need to say them (see D&C 100:5–6). The more talks we give in sacrament meeting and in lessons, the better we'll be as teachers.

The greatest calling on this earth is to teach. You remember that Alma was the chief judge but he conferred the chief judgeship seat upon Nephihah so he could teach. He said he had to go out and teach all the people by bearing pure testimony (see Alma 4:18–19). What do mothers and fathers do? They teach. It is the highest and noblest calling, and when we teach the word of God, there's nothing better, because we help people come unto Christ and enjoy happiness.

Many of you will have missionary preparation courses in your ward and in your stakes, and that is good. You can take Religion 130, Missionary Preparation, at all of the Church colleges and institutes of religion.

Learn some domestic skills; learn how to cook and wash and iron and clean. And you know what you sisters and elders can do? Check out the videos *Called to Serve* and *Labor of Love* from your ward library. There are other great videos like *Heavenly Father's Plan, What Is Real,* and *Together Forever,* to name a few. They will help you prepare to become good missionaries.

There are usually missionaries wherever you live. Go on a "teach" with the missionaries. They will let you read a scripture, bear your testimony, or just smile a lot—it's OK. It doesn't hurt one bit; it's a great feeling and you will love it. Especially those of you who are retired. If you want a great experience, go as a senior missionary. (P.S. You younger missionaries get your grandparents to serve.) When I was a mission president I was so grateful for every senior missionary. They were the leaven of our mission. What they did was indescribably delicious. They brought people back to church who were less active. They were a strength to the young missionaries. They were just the greatest. You never want to stop being missionaries for the Lord. In fact, when people ask where you served, you just say, "earth." Every day is a missionary day in your life.

RELATIONSHIPS

We must learn how to build up relationships so people will trust, love, and respect us. That's the first thing we do as missionaries— build relationships of trust. We need to learn how to talk to people and build up a relationship where they will trust, love, and respect us to a point that they will allow us to teach them the gospel. We must be an example, because what we are speaks so loudly, people often don't hear a word we say. We teach what we are. If we're full of love, they'll want to listen to us. Relationships are the key. Our children will not listen until they trust, love, and respect us. We must learn to be true and honest friends. Then people will trust us to the point where we can teach them.

OVERCOMING TEMPTATION

There are some things you need to be aware of. Temptation is real, and Satan desireth to sift you as wheat. You must pray every day to avoid and overcome temptation (see 3 Ne. 18:15,18). Temptation is real. When you put in your papers, temptation becomes greater. When you get your call, temptation increases. You must remember the Lord needs you. You must overcome temptation with charity, with faith, with humility, with the word of God, and with the Spirit as you pray with all your heart, might, mind, and soul.

CONCLUSION

This is the day to prepare. Prepare every needful thing so you can be an instrument in the hands of the Lord to bring souls unto Christ and taste of the exceeding great joy (see Alma 36:24).

✥ CHAPTER 3 ✥

RECOGNIZING YOUR CAPACITY AND POTENTIAL AS A MISSIONARY

You are a set-apart missionary. You are a disciple of Jesus Christ. Elder Bruce R. McConkie has said of your commission:

> I am called of God. My authority is above that of the kings of the earth. By revelation I have been selected as a personal representative of the Lord Jesus Christ. He is my Master and He has chosen me to represent Him. To stand in His place, to say and do what He himself would say and do if He personally were ministering to the very people to whom He has sent me. My voice is His voice, and my acts are His acts; my words are His words and my doctrine is His doctrine. My commission is to do what He wants done. To say what He wants said. To be a living modern witness in word and deed of the divinity of His great and marvelous latter-day work (address delivered while serving as president of the Australian Mission, 1961–64).

AMBASSADORS OF CHRIST

As missionaries and missionary leaders we talk of Christ, we preach of Christ, we testify of Christ. All of us who are serving the Lord in the mission field are His disciples and ambassadors. The light that we hold is the Lord Jesus Christ (see 3 Ne. 18:24). As Elder Hans B. Ringger so eloquently explains:

> The foundation and guiding light for all our decisions is the gospel of Jesus Christ and His message to the world. The teach-

ings of Christ must be embedded in our desire to choose the right and in our wish to find happiness. His righteous life must be reflected in our own actions. The Lord not only teaches love, He *is* love. He not only preached the importance of faith, repentance, baptism, and the gift of the Holy Ghost, He *lived* accordingly. His life reflected the gospel that He preached. There was and is total harmony between His thoughts and His actions ("Choose You This Day," *Ensign*, May 1990, 25).

We cannot bear testimony of this Church and this kingdom without knowing Jesus Christ, the Savior of the world. When we know Christ, we can hold up His light; He is the light and the life of the world (see John 8:12). And when we hold up that light, then we truly become His disciples.

In 3 Nephi Jesus Christ tells His disciples that they are "the light of this people" (3 Ne. 12:14), and He explains that they will bless all of Heavenly Father's children. Christ instructs the Nephites not to put their light under a bushel, but to put it "on a candlestick, and it giveth light to all that are in the house" (3 Ne. 12:15). That same instruction applies to each of us: when we possess the light of Jesus Christ, we must not put it under a bushel. That light must be held up, and then—and only then—will we be true and worthy representatives of our Savior, Jesus Christ.

President Gordon B. Hinckley observed that we represent Christ's army:

> In this work there must be commitment. There must be devotion. We are engaged in a great eternal struggle that concerns the very souls of the sons and daughters of God. We are not losing. We are winning. We will continue to win if we will be faithful and true. We can do it. We must do it. We will do it. There is nothing the Lord has asked of us that in faith we cannot accomplish ("The War We Are Winning," *Ensign*, Nov. 1986, 44).

We are charged to be His soldiers, to find and help save our brothers and sisters. Each one of us needs help. Sister Pinegar's my keeper, and she works hard to help me do what's right. I pray that each of you will seek to be shepherds like Christ, to be your brothers' and sisters' keeper, and as you work to help each other, remember: "Inasmuch as ye have done it unto one of the least of these my brethren, ye have done it unto me" (Matt. 25:40).

We must not be manipulative salespeople. We must be disciples of Christ. All the knowledge and skills we learn must be magnified by the power of God, by the attributes of Christ, by the Spirit of the Lord, by the mind and will of the Lord.

THE POWER OF THE HOLY GHOST

If I would pray for anything for the missionaries scattered all over the world, I would pray that the Spirit of the Lord would come upon them with such power that they would never, ever want to do anything wrong again. When we're filled with the power of the Holy Ghost, we simply cannot sin. That's why the Nephite nation, in 3 Nephi 19:9, prayed "for that which they most desired; and they desired that the Holy Ghost should be given unto them."

Why would the Nephites desire the Holy Ghost so fervently? Elder Parley P. Pratt answered this question when he described the extraordinary characteristics of this remarkable power:

> The gift of the Holy Spirit . . . quickens all the intellectual faculties, increases, enlarges, expands, and purifies all the natural passions and affections; and adapts them, by the gift of wisdom, to their lawful use . . . It inspires virtue, kindness, goodness, tenderness, gentleness, and charity. It develops beauty of person, form and features. It tends to health, vigor, animation, and social feeling. It develops and invigorates all the faculties of the physical and intellectual man. It strengthens, invigorates, and gives tone to the nerves. In short, it is, as it were, marrow to the bone, joy to the heart, light to the eyes, music to the ears, and life to the whole being (*Key to the Science of Theology*, 100–102).

So all you need for a strong testimony is the companionship of the Holy Ghost. Just because you can't move a mountain yet, don't ever think your testimony isn't strong, because it is. Every testimony that's born is not born of man, but born of God by the power of the

Holy Ghost. When we bear testimony it's not you or me—it's the Spirit of God, and that's powerful.

Just the other day I got a letter. "Dear President Pinegar," it started, "We didn't know what we were doing. We didn't know which way was up, but we took ten copies of the Book of Mormon, we placed ten copies, and we have nine referrals. Is that pretty good?"

Pretty good? This elder didn't know all the dialogues. He didn't know every word to say. But he loved the Lord and loved the person he was talking to, and when he bore testimony of the Book of Mormon, that testimony went into the other person's heart. "For when a man speaketh by the power of the Holy Ghost the power of the Holy Ghost carrieth it unto the hearts of the children of men" (2 Ne. 33:1).

Each missionary has been called of God. Do you understand the magnitude of that? You've taken upon yourself sacred covenants. You've been empowered from on high. In my eyes, you're wonderful. If you abhor sin, and you are like Nephi of old, you will with unwearyingness want to be obedient. With unwearyingness you will want to be kind to your companion, even when he or she doesn't deserve it. With unwearyingness you'll say your prayers; you'll do every needful thing. With unwearyingness and perseverance you'll do those things you've covenanted to do (see Hel. 10:4–6).

As missionaries, you must teach the Lord's word from His book, for these are the scriptures of the Restoration. When you look into the eyes of your investigators and testify, "It's true, I beg of you to read it. I testify," then they will believe.

You enter the mission field to find, teach, and baptize. There is no hope for anyone on this earth unless they receive the covenants of the priesthood of God through baptism and the holy temple. You can be friendly and kind and loving, and that is good. But you must testify with power to bring people to Christ—the Spirit is that power.

HUMILITY AND SPIRITUAL GROWTH

As part of the perfection process, the Book of Mormon instructs us that we must be humble or we will not learn (see 2 Ne. 9:42). And in Ether we are told that becoming humble is part of the process of learning, recognizing our weaknesses, and becoming strong and great in the Lord's hands. Humility is essential to that process:

> And if men come unto me I will show unto them their weakness. I give unto men weakness that they may be humble; and my grace is sufficient for all men that humble themselves before me; for if they humble themselves before me, and have faith in me, then will I make weak things become strong unto them (Ether 12:27).

Certainly the people in the Book of Mormon had a hard time with humility, and we have a hard time, too. But we are told that when God loves a people, He chastens them (see Hebrews 12:6). Chastening often results in humility, and we cannot grow without humility.

Humility is the beginning virtue or the precursor of all spiritual growth. Until we are humble, we cannot grow. Elder Richard G. Scott describes this virtue in even greater detail:

> Humility is the precious, fertile soil of righteous character. It germinates the seeds of personal growth. When cultivated through the exercise of faith, pruned by repentance, and fortified by obedience and good works, such seeds produce the cherished fruit of spirituality (see Alma 26:22). Divine inspiration and power then result. Inspiration is to know the will of the Lord. Power is the capability to accomplish that inspired will (See D&C 43:15–16). Such power comes from God after we have done "all we can do" (see 2 Ne. 25:23) ("The Plan for Happiness and Exaltation," *Ensign*, Nov. 1981, 11).

You recall when Alma was teaching the Zoramites; many were humbled because they were cast out of the synagogue. And it was those who were cast out of the synagogue who listened to Alma and his message (see Alma 31–32). The wealthy and haughty Zoramites, those climbing up on the Rameumptom and praying, did not hear the word of God or feel the Spirit of the Lord. Humility is the key to our ability. As missionaries, your hearts will resonate to President Lorenzo Snow's observation:

> The Lord has not chosen the great and learned of the world
> to perform His work on the earth . . . but humble men [and
> women] devoted to His cause . . . who are willing to be led and
> guided by the Holy Spirit, and who will of necessity give the
> glory unto Him knowing that of themselves they can do
> nothing" (*Teachings of Lorenzo Snow*, 77).

Humility leads to righteousness and goodness. That's why I just love to be around missionaries, teaching them, because missionaries are so willing to accept the teachings of the Lord. I tingle when I think what a great honor and joy it is to work among the missionaries; their righteousness and willingness is inspiring and touching.

I think of two missionaries in specific, a companionship I worked with when I was mission president. These two elders were my assistants. "President," they said, "we've only got a month left. We're training the new assistants, and they're doing really well. President, please let us go teach and baptize." In other words, they didn't want the honor of being assistants to the president or any other honors of men. "Let us just go find and teach," they said. "President, we feel the power of God is upon us." And with that commitment and their strong desire, they went out and joyfully baptized twenty-three people in one month.

How was that possible? Simple: it happened because of the humility of two missionaries who gave themselves to the Lord and asked every day, "Father, what would thou have us do?" And then they went out and did it.

Of course, no matter how great we are, it doesn't mean we don't need to change. None of us are perfect. But it does mean that we are willing to serve, and that we are submitting to the Lord—giving Him the gift of our hearts. Whenever the people in the Book of Mormon were prideful or disobedient, the Lord would work with them to bring about humility so they could grow. Sometimes if the people were doing well, the Lord would send prophets who would exhort them to be better. Sometimes they became wicked, sinking into sinful behavior, and the Lord would still exhort them. Sometimes the people would change, and sometimes they wouldn't. Our challenge is to learn from their experiences and always be willing to change.

EVALUATING OUR LIVES AND BECOMING LIKE CHRIST

We grow and become like Christ through recognizing where we are and what we need to do. Once we evaluate our lives, we set goals and make plans to keep the commandments and the covenants we have made. Unfortunately, some of us never recognize where we are because we never take the time to evaluate our lives. Every day should be an evaluating day, a goal-setting and plan-making day, and a living day.

In Alma 5, Alma the Younger asks the people to consider at least forty-three questions about their spiritual progress. Can you imagine the scene?

Alma was speaking by way of commandment to Church members, reminding them of the goodness of God in their lives. He asked the people (and I'm paraphrasing), "Has a remembrance of the captivity of your fathers brought you to remember the mercy and long-suffering of God towards you? Do you realize He delivered your soul from hell?" Alma 5 is the great evaluation chapter—a great example of the questions we can ask ourselves as we're evaluating our own lives.

Alma continues, reminding the people that God "changed their hearts; yea, he awakened them out of a deep sleep, and they awoke unto God. Behold, they were in the midst of darkness; nevertheless, their souls were illuminated by the light of the everlasting word" (v. 7). Our souls, too, are illuminated by the everlasting word.

"Yea," Alma continues, "they were encircled about by the bands of death, and the chains of hell, and an everlasting destruction did await them" (v. 7).

And then Alma talks about experiencing a mighty change of heart, and asks those in the congregation if they had been spiritually born of God (see v. 14).

Can you imagine that? He's talking to Church members (like us), asking if they realize that it's not enough to just be baptized and receive the Holy Ghost; he's saying that we must be spiritually born of God.

In verse 13 Alma observes:

> And behold, [Alma the Elder] preached the word unto your fathers, and a mighty change was also wrought in their hearts,

and they humbled themselves and put their trust in the true and living God. And behold, they were faithful until the end; therefore they were saved."

Notice how it is humility, being meek and lowly, that creates a place for the word in our hearts, and the word then brings a willingness to change.

There are more treasures in Alma 5. Through the spirit of revelation, Alma asks the people if they've been stripped of envy and pride. He asks who mocks or persecutes others. Listen to the fate of someone who belittles another one of Heavenly Father's children: "Wo unto such an one, for he is not prepared, and the time is at hand that he must repent or he cannot be saved!" (v. 31).

Alma pleads with all of his heart, and I plead with all of my heart, that we all might listen to the words of Christ and examine ourselves as suggested in Alma 5.

As did Alma, I also speak by way of command to you, the disciples of Christ. We must honestly look at ourselves and evaluate our lives and actions. Each day we can say, "I am a divine child of God, and I can be better each day, a step at a time." Don't overwhelm yourself; but whether you're nineteen or ninety-nine, each day strive to be better than you were the day before.

Oh, you missionaries are so good! You'll increase in your faith because you'll have a vision of who you are. You'll possess the pure love of Christ because you know who you are. You'll choose to be exactly obedient because you love your God.

Each day I pray that you'll take a moment to look in the mirror (maybe the mirror could even have a picture of Christ taped to it) and evaluate your life. Then go and do as Jesus would do. Every day, let us be as the Savior, Jesus Christ, would have us be. And what manner of men and women ought we to be? The Savior tells us: "Therefore I would that ye should be perfect even as I, or your Father who is in heaven is perfect" (3 Ne. 12:48).

CONCLUSION

Now is the time, and you are the ones who are instruments in the hands of God to bring souls unto Christ. I love you; I honor you. I thank God that you are here to carry the gospel to His children upon the earth. May God bless you in your endeavors to do so.

⇌ $\mathscr{C}$HAPTER 4 ⇌

ATTAINING GOSPEL KNOWLEDGE

It's important to understand many doctrines, concepts, and teachings that will help you be a better representative of our Savior, Jesus Christ. If you study and teach the following eight doctrines, your own testimony will grow, and you will be a better instrument in the Lord's hands to help His children understand, appreciate, and accept the gospel in their lives.

THE ATONEMENT

The first doctrine is the Atonement of Christ, the center of the gospel of Jesus Christ.

> And this is the gospel, the glad tidings, which the voice out of the heavens bore record unto us—That he came into the world, even Jesus, to be crucified for the world, and to bear the sins of the world, and to sanctify the world, and to cleanse it from all unrighteousness (D&C 76:40–41).

This is the Atonement. He suffered that we might live. He sweat great drops of blood that we might be made pure. He died on the cross that we might live again, and the principles of the Atonement that help us live again are the first principles of the gospel: faith in the Lord Jesus Christ, repentance through the Lord Jesus Christ, baptism and taking upon ourselves the name of Jesus Christ, and the blessings of the Holy Ghost.

If we read 2 Nephi 9, we'll understand the Atonement like we've never understood it before. Our gratitude will deepen. We'll recognize what we would have been had there been no Atonement. Now, how can the Atonement help us?

> And he shall go forth, suffering pains and afflictions and temptations of every kind; and this that the word might be fulfilled which saith he will take upon him the pains and the sicknesses of his people. And he will take upon him death, that he may loose the bands of death which bind his people; and he will take upon him their infirmities, that his bowels may be filled with mercy, according to the flesh, that he may know according to the flesh how to succor his people according to their infirmities (Alma 7:11–12).

The Atonement of Christ nurtures and blesses us through the grace of God. It helps us repent. We can overcome sin through repentance because of the grace of God and the atoning sacrifice. Sin separates us from the Father; we lose the Spirit, and we separate ourselves. The law of justice demands sin be paid for. The law of mercy provides a way, through God's only begotten Son, to pay for our sins. Everything must be paid for. Earth life was not free. We knew that in our premortal life. Everything has a price, but everything is a gift of God. Exaltation has a price—the grace of God after all we can do (see 2 Ne. 25:23). What is "all we can do?" We can obey; but when we don't obey, we must pay the price of repentance. You see, every needful thing has a price, and the Atonement of Jesus Christ our Savior is a price He paid to fulfill the demands of divine justice.

D&C 19:15–21 teaches us what price we must pay if we don't repent. If we do not repent, the Lord said we must suffer even as He has suffered; for the Atonement, as it relates to exaltation, requires that we must repent. The Atonement freely gives us immortality; we all gain immortality, but eternal life comes only by applying the Atonement in our life, through repentance and endurance to the end. In repentance is also forgiveness. In other words, if we do not forgive, we do not repent; we do not take advantage of the Atonement in our lives.

Write in your journal today what you're going to do to show gratitude to the Savior for His atoning sacrifice. Your list of commitments can be lived every day, and you can make a covenant with the Lord in regard to your behavior because of His infinite, atoning sacrifice.

FAITH

Faith has three degrees: hope and belief, action, and power. You've read the definition of faith in Alma 32 and Hebrews 11: "Faith is the substance of things hoped for." That is the first degree of faith. James said, "I will shew thee my faith by my works"—meaning action (James 2:18). The brother of Jared "said unto the mountain Zerin, Remove"—meaning power (Ether 12:30). If you want to read more on faith as power, then read the Lectures on Faith by the Prophet Joseph Smith, and you'll begin to understand.

Faith is power, power to do all things. The earth was created by faith. Faith is the vehicle of the priesthood. Faith is the foundation of all righteousness.

Joseph Smith taught that before we can exercise faith, we must know the character of God: know that He exists, know that He is perfect, know that we are actually living according to the will of God. We cannot please God without faith (see Hebrews 11:6). You cannot exercise faith without love, and you can't have love without faith (see Gal. 5:6). Faith, love, and obedience are intertwined. You cannot separate one from another. The greater our faith, the more we will love God, and if we love Him we will obey Him. The Lord said, if you love me, keep my commandments (see John 14:15). If we have faith, we will mentally and spiritually exert ourselves and draw upon the powers of heaven.

The question is left for us to answer: what kind of lives are we living because of the Savior Jesus Christ? When we look at our lives, remember—they are only a reflection of our conversion to Jesus Christ, of our faith in Him.

PROPHETS AND REVELATION

The third doctrine we need to understand concerns the prophets of God, the spokesmen for the Lord Jesus Christ. "Surely the Lord God will do nothing, but he revealeth his secret unto his servants the prophets" (Amos 3:7). Prophets speak for our Savior. They speak the words of Christ. The Lord said, in Doctrine and Covenants 1:38, "Whether by mine own voice or by the voice of my servants, it is the same." The Prophet functions as the President of the Church, the presiding high priest, and the revelator of the Church for the Lord Jesus Christ. The Quorum of the Twelve and Council of the First Presidency are also prophets, seers, and revelators. They speak for the Lord.

In addition to that, the fact is that every person should be a prophet for himself and in his own concerns. It was Moses who said: "Would God that all the Lord's people were prophets, and that the Lord would put his spirit upon them" (Num. 11:29). It was Paul who said we should "covet to prophesy" (1 Cor. 14:39). In other words, you can be a prophet for your own soul, receiving revelation from God on things you should do, remembering always that the Prophet of the Church is the only one who receives revelation for the Church and kingdom of God upon the earth.

Remember, it is our duty to sustain the Prophet, which means to support—to follow—what he has asked us to do. In the battle against the offender Amalek, the Israelites under Joshua prevailed as long as Moses' hands were outstretched on the top of the hill, supported on either side by Aaron and Hur (see Ex. 17:9–13). Thus we see the importance of noble "counselors" in the grand program of God's kingdom. Similarly, Moses was able to sustain the awesome burden of presiding over so vast a people as the Israelites only because his father-in-law, Jethro, wisely taught him the art and practice of careful delegation and prioritizing of the work (see Ex. 18:17–26). This wonderful example helps us realize how important Church members are in regards to sustaining the Prophet and assisting in building up the kingdom of God.

How grateful we should be for a prophet, a living prophet of God. I bear testimony to you, that as we follow the Prophets we will never be led astray.

THE DIVINE CALLING OF JOSEPH SMITH

The fourth doctrine concerns the divine calling of the Prophet Joseph Smith. How do you feel about the Prophet Joseph? "Joseph Smith, the Prophet and Seer of the Lord, has done more, save Jesus only, for the salvation of men in this world, than any other man that ever lived in it" (D&C 135:3). He was the prophet of the Restoration. He spoke for the Lord; he gave us the Book of Mormon, the Doctrine and Covenants, the Pearl of Great Price, and the inspired version of the Holy Bible. He established the kingdom as the Lord directed him.

We must bear testimony that Joseph Smith was the prophet of the Restoration. He holds the keys for the dispensation of the fullness of times. He is the prophet that stands at the head. When we think of all that the Prophet Joseph Smith has done, we will be grateful and recognize that our life is what it is today because of the revelations he received from our Savior by the power of the Holy Ghost.

Think of all the persecution that was heaped upon him. He was tarred and feathered and left for dead in Hyrum, Ohio; he was beaten, thrown in jail, and finally martyred. Can anyone doubt the blessings of the gospel in our life because of what Joseph Smith did? He literally fulfilled the measure of his creation because of his integrity and love. In fact, when people ask why Joseph Smith was so great, the answer comes back that he was full of the love of Christ— so much so, that even the day after he was tarred and feathered he gave a talk on forgiveness and repentance; and some of the men who had done the deed were in attendance.

When you pray to Heavenly Father, you will know, as I know, that Joseph is the prophet of the Restoration, and the Church is led by a prophet today.

THE TRUTHFULNESS OF THE BOOK OF MORMON

The fifth important doctrine is the truthfulness of the Book of Mormon. The Book of Mormon is the keystone of our religion; the fullness of the gospel is in its printed pages. It is the word of God and the truest book, it will help us to get closer to God than any other book (see "Introduction," Book of Mormon). The Book of Mormon is true, of that I testify. It is a record of the dealings of God with man. And the purpose of the book is to show the goodness and mercies of God to His people, and above all, to teach that Jesus is the Christ, the Son of the living God.

As President Heber J. Grant said,

> I am convinced in my own mind, my dear brethren and
> sisters, that this book, the Book of Mormon, is the greatest
> converter of men and women as to the divinity of the gospel of
> Jesus Christ. It is in every way a true witness of God, and it
> sustains the Bible and is in harmony with the Bible (qtd. by
> Joseph L. Wirthlin, Conference Report, April 1947, 84).

If all of us, when placing the Book of Mormon, would carefully read the
testimonies inside to our investigators, and then bear witness, giving it as we
would a priceless gift, we would find that people would read it more carefully and would realize its importance in their lives.

The Book of Mormon—oh, how I love the book. For twenty-
seven glorious years I've had the privilege of teaching that book at
BYU and the Orem Institute of Religion. It made a difference in my
family's life. When we read it on a daily basis it made us start to live
the word of God. There are legions of people who have read the book
and then requested baptism because of the power of its words. The
Spirit carries it unto the hearts of the people. And the true seekers,
the Lord's elect, will believe.

When you study the Book of Mormon today, remember to apply
its teachings to your own life. Every teaching in the Book of
Mormon is to be applied to life. The Prophet Nephi said, "I did
liken all scripture unto us . . . for our profit and learning" (1 Ne.
19:23). Put the promise of the book to the test—pray to know of its
truthfulness (see Moroni 10:4–5). It is true. It is the truest book of
all books. The Book of Mormon is the word of God and will bring
people to Christ.

THE HOLY GHOST

The sixth doctrine is the Holy Ghost. When the Savior was
preaching to the people in the Nephite nation, they prayed for that
which they desired more than anything else, that they might have the
gift of the Holy Ghost (see 3 Ne. 19:9). Why did they pray for the

Holy Ghost? Why did they desire to have it so much? Because, as Elder Bruce R. McConkie tells us:

> He is the Comforter, Testator, Revelator, Sanctifier, Holy Spirit, Holy Spirit of Promise, Spirit of Truth, Spirit of the Lord, and Messenger of the Father and the Son, and His companionship is the greatest gift that mortal man can enjoy (*Mormon Doctrine*, 359).

In addition to general faith, love, and obedience, four specific things will invite the Spirit into our lives: (1) searching the scriptures, (2) fasting and praying, (3) giving righteous service and (4) building up the kingdom of God. As we give righteous service, remember, our personal righteousness is the greatest gift we can give the Lord, and it sets a special example for those we are trying to teach. We cannot have the Spirit without righteousness, and we cannot teach save we have the Spirit (see D&C 42:14).

The Holy Ghost must be with us as we teach. The Holy Ghost will bear witness to anyone that the gospel is true. In Galatians we read about receiving the spirit of love, peace, joy, long-suffering, gentleness, goodness, faith, meekness and temperance (see 5:22–23); all these are fruits of the Spirit. When we feel good, we are feeling the influence of the Spirit. In D&C 11:12–13, the Lord talks about the Spirit again. He says that it will lead us to do good, to be humble, to deal justly, to judge righteously. It will enlighten our souls and bring us joy. Yes, the fruits of the Spirit will help us recognize the Spirit and to identify it for others so we can help them know the gospel is true.

Recognizing the Spirit of God in our life is no different than asking investigators to recognize the Spirit. Don't look beyond the mark. You need not have a burning bush. A simple feeling of peace and a desire to do good should be enough. The Holy Ghost will be a comfort and a guide, and direct you in every way. The Lord will not leave you alone as you prepare every needful thing to bless the lives of your fellowmen and build up the kingdom of God.

PRAYER

The seventh doctrine is prayer. Sometimes missionaries say, "Well I just don't get an answer President," or "My investigators just don't get answers when they pray." Heavenly Father teaches us that we must study it out to know of its truthfulness; and then we need to make a decision (see D&C 9:7–9). Then we take that decision to the Lord and He will cause our bosom to burn. Sometimes we'll just feel peace, as He said to Oliver, "Did I not speak peace to your mind?" (D&C 6:23). Remember all those other feelings of the Spirit? We will feel good, we will be humble, and we'll have a desire to deal justly with others. These are the feelings that will tell you that the gospel is true. But, as with Oliver in section 9, the Lord says, "You took no thought save it was to ask me" (v. 7). You don't just ask. You ask with real intent, having faith, having done the things you need to do, and then your prayer will be answered. In other words, prayers are answered when we do our part. We just cannot say, "Give me, give me, give me," but we must come before our Lord, our God, with all our heart, might, mind, and strength, having faith with real intent, and then He will answer our prayers, either directly or through others.

Prayer is communicating with our Heavenly Father in the name of Jesus Christ. That is the way you pray. It is through and in the name of Jesus Christ. In 3 Nephi 18, we note that the Savior continually told the Nephites to pray in His own name; that is so we may know that it is through Jesus Christ, our advocate and mediator, that God our Father helps us. Know this: God hears and answers prayers. Pray with real intent, without vain repetitions, with a sincere heart, having faith, and with every needful thing in place.

We can pray standing up, we can be walking along on the street, we can be leaning against a building; and the Lord said that when we cease our prayers, we should have a prayer in our hearts (see 3 Ne. 20:1). Our prayers must be sent up to heaven continually. Prayer is the very essence of knowing and worshiping our Heavenly Father. We must take the time to know our Father through prayer.

Always remember to use Thee, Thou, and Thine to show reverence. Remember always to pray to have the courage to do the will of the Father. Pray: "Father, bless me that I might do thy will."

TESTIMONY

The eighth doctrine pertains to the power of testimony. Bearing and receiving testimony is the act of imparting knowledge as you receive it by revelation from the Holy Ghost. This is testimony. No one can really be a minister of the Lord Jesus Christ, except he has a testimony that Jesus is the Christ.

Our testimony, when truly born, is born by the power of the Holy Ghost. That makes our testimonies as strong as any man's upon the earth, because true testimonies are only born by the power of the Spirit. So when we are bearing witness of the truthfulness of the gospel, the truthfulness of the Book of Mormon, the truthfulness of the prophet, the truthfulness of the teachings, yea, the truthfulness of the kingdom of God on the earth, we do this by the power and authority of the Holy Ghost. The Holy Ghost is the testator, it is the revelator, and it is only by the Holy Ghost that we can testify to the truthfulness of the knowledge that Jesus is the Christ, the Son of God, and that The Church of Jesus Christ of Latter-day Saints is the true kingdom of God on the earth.

Can you see now that one of the most priceless possessions we have is our testimony? Bearing testimony is testifying of revealed eternal truths in the gospel of Jesus Christ.

How do we get a testimony? Study, pray, live it, and bear it. Isn't that interesting? What do we ask investigators to do? Study, pray, and live the commandments. You see, we do everything by eternal truths. Nothing we ask of nonmembers is by happenstance. How many prophets have preached those same doctrines? To gain a testimony we must study, pray, live it, and bear it, and then we'll know. President Hinckley reaffirms this for us:

> If there are any [of you] lacking that testimony, you can get it; and you must get it . . . The Lord has said that he that doeth the will of the Father shall know of the doctrine, "whether it be of God, or whether I speak of myself" (John 7:17) (*Teachings of Gordon B. Hinckley*, 647).

When we bear our testimonies they are strengthened because we're invoking the Holy Ghost. The more experiences we have with the Holy Ghost, the stronger our testimonies become. Sometimes it is given to us to have a testimony on the words of others (see D&C 46:14); and until our testimony is strong enough, sometimes we have to do that. Everything we have is a gift of God, and this testimony that we possess, no matter how small, or how great, is a gift from God. Think of the times when other people's testimonies have affected yours. Think of the times other people have been affected by your testimony. The greatest converting power is the converting power of testimony, the word of God as given by the Spirit. Testimony is the purest form of the word; the power of the word has greater power to change men's lives than anything else (see Alma 31:5). The power of the word makes a difference in testimony. Testify. Truth without testimony is hollow. The gospel is true, and we are the instruments through which He works to share the truth with every nation, kindred, tongue, and people.

CONCLUSION

When we come to understand and appreciate the doctrines and principles we will be filled with gratitude. Gratitude is a catalyst of change. Our attitudes and behaviors will change as these doctrines are integrated and become part of our very being. As President Boyd K. Packer has said, "The study of the doctrines of the gospel will improve behavior quicker than a study of behavior will improve behavior." ("Little Children," Ensign, Nov. 1986, 16). Knowledge truly is power.

~ CHAPTER 5 ~

HAVING A GREAT DAY ON YOUR MISSION

Every day can be a great day on your mission. You can choose to have a great day on your mission because Heavenly Father and our Savior will help you. You are responsible and accountable for your life. The consequences and rewards are yours. And the Spirit will direct you so you can have a great day today. So let's get started with how to do that.

BE SINGLE-MINDED

The first thing to remember is that we came to this earth to do the will of our Father. In the premortal councils we agreed we would come and do our best to return to God's presence by doing His will. To accomplish this, we cannot have one foot in the world and one foot in the kingdom. It is impossible. Our eyes must be single to the glory of our Father.

We must be single-minded. We must leave our cares at home in the hands of our Heavenly Father (see D&C 100:1–2). If our eye is single to His glory, our whole body will be filled with light, and the light is the Lord Jesus Christ (see D&C 88:67). That's what gives us power. If we ever, ever lose the desire to do the will of the Father, we will have a very difficult time on our mission. Like Nephi of old, He will prepare a way for us to accomplish the things He commands us to do (see 1 Ne.3:7). Ammon knew where his strength came from: "I know that I am nothing," but "in his strength I can do all things" (see Alma 26:12). Yes, if we agree to do the will of the Father, our Father will strengthen us.

I love Abinadi. To me, Abinadi was the epitome of the great missionary because he practiced the doctrine of doing the will of the Father. As you recall the story, King Noah was leading his people astray. Abinadi was sent there to preach and they tried to kill him, but he said (I'm paraphrasing here), "It mattereth not what you do to me and my body, but I will do the will of the Father. I have come to preach the word, and after that, do whatever you will" (see Mosiah 13:3–9). They burned Abinadi at the stake. He was a martyr. His validation wasn't a name-brand clothing label—or any other temporal thing—that said, "I'm OK, I'm important." His validation came from the Father because he did the Father's will. We probably won't be asked to die for the kingdom, but rather to live for it.

The only validation that matters is our Heavenly Father's approval of what we have done. Doing the will of the Father is the first great step toward having a great day on your mission, for He will validate you and give you strength, and you will feel good. If our mind is not single to His glory, and if we have our own agenda, we are in trouble whether we're a missionary or not, because our own agenda dictates our behavior. That's why we pray to Heavenly Father to direct our paths. Lead me, guide me, walk beside me. The Liahona—the word of God—is our director. The word of God is a representation of Christ. Yes, everything ties in to doing the will of the Father. Once that is entrenched, every day will become a great day.

LEARN TO PLAN

How do you begin to have a great day? You have to plan. You've heard the old cliché, "If you fail to plan, you plan to fail." Organize every needful thing (see D&C 88:119). If you do not plan well, it is very difficult to have a good day. Too often we just put out brush fires because we fail to make an overall plan. The principle of planning is eternal. The principle of organizing is eternal. Joseph Smith taught that Genesis describes the creation of the earth with the Hebrew word Barau, meaning "to organize" (The Words of Joseph Smith: The Contemporary Accounts of the Nauvoo Discourses of the Prophet Joseph, eds. Andrew F. Ehat and Lyndon W. Cook [Provo: BYU

Religious Studies Center, 1980], 397). So organizing means creating. You can "create" a wonderful mission.

Create a great day by planning. Have a vision of what you want to be, and how you plan to accomplish that. Do you have a vision of what you should radiate? Have you made a mission statement about what kind of missionary you're going to be? Do you have a plan as a missionary to find souls every day? Every moment of every day is a finding moment. Do you have a plan to teach with power by the Spirit? Do you have a plan to help your investigators progress by making and keeping commitments? Do you have a plan to help keep them active? Do you have a plan to help the less active? Do you have a plan to not only place copies of the Book of Mormon, but get promises to read them? Do you have a plan to serve your companions—to be nice to them and say, "I'll make breakfast today," or, "Your shoes look a little tattered, why don't I polish them for you tonight?" You are thinking I'm crazy, nobody does things like that. But there are missionaries who are like that. There are missionaries who care because they have the love of God and they make a plan that shows they care.

If you do not plan, the river of life will just take you any way it's going. And so will your mission. Whatever is happening, you'll just follow the flow. You need a plan. Plan to always show love. Four hours a week are designated to give service, Christian service, to go out and do something to help somebody else. That's part of the plan. Isn't that interesting? The Prophet says that missionaries in the full-time service of the Lord should be sure to take four hours a week and give unsolicited Christian service. Oh, I love the Prophet. He reveals truth to us, and every thing we receive from him is literally a plan from God.

Be a planner. Be administratively sound so you can be spiritually in tune. I like that. Be administratively sound so you can be spiritually in tune. If your apartment is dirty, and your clothes are hanging all over the place, and there are pots in the sink and your clothes aren't ready for the day . . . then you just kind of feel yucky and that means you're not administratively sound. If everything is in its place, you'll be surprised how easy it is to be spiritually in tune. Organize yourself, then you will never be rushing around inefficiently, for you are prepared for the day.

PRAY

Plan to pray. Pray with all your heart, might, mind, and soul for direction, for strength, for courage, for your investigators, and for people to love and to serve. It's a key to a great day. Prayer is so powerful that all of the great gifts of God—revelations, faith, humility, charity, and so many more—come as a result of prayer. Remember James 1:5, "If any of you lack wisdom, let him ask of God." Joseph Smith asked Heavenly Father, and what was the result? The first vision. Lehi received the vision to leave Jerusalem when he asked Heavenly Father. Section 138, that glorious vision about the redemption of all who have died without a knowledge of the gospel, was a result of Joseph F. Smith asking about the scriptures. Joseph Smith, reading the Gospel of John, asked Heavenly Father about the resurrection of souls. The result was D&C 76. If we don't ask in prayer, we take away one of the greatest blessings of our lives—revelation and direction from our Heavenly Father.

I'll never forget a conversation with Truman Madsen as I was coming out of my Book of Mormon class; I looked at him and said, "Tru, what is the greatest need in the Church today?" And I just wondered what he would say, because he's so wonderful and kind and sweet and brilliant and bald, and all those wonderful things. And he said, "Ed," and he took about one second, and finished, "prayer." You think about prayer. Without it we cannot have charity.

You want to have a great day on your mission? Be full of love. "Pray unto the Father with all the energy of heart, that ye may be filled with [His] love" (Moroni 7:48). When fast Sunday comes around next month, what are we going to do? We're going to pray and fast for charity, for faith, and for our investigators. Fast and pray for things that will make you a better instrument in the hands of the Lord.

HUMILITY

What about our humility? Humility is being totally dependent upon God and developing a relationship with him. The fruits of humility are being submissive, meek, lowly, patient and teachable. These are the qualities that help us realize we're totally dependent upon God; and at that point we can begin to have a relationship with Him. Prayer is the personification of our humility. For example, when we say, "Heavenly Father," we've acknowledged our relationship— child and parent. When we say, "We ask thee," we show our dependence upon Him. Isn't that wonderful? Humility is personified through our prayers, and as we pray we will be full of humility and faith. "They did fast and pray oft, and did wax stronger and stronger in their humility, and firmer and firmer in [their] faith" (Hel. 3:35).

TEMPTATION AND OBEDIENCE

As we've learned, if we're going to be great missionaries we need to have charity, humility, and faith. Isn't it interesting that all those come through prayer? And all of those, especially prayer, help us resist temptation. As missionaries, to have a great day, we've got to avoid temptation. Watch and pray always lest ye are tempted (see 3 Ne. 18:15,18). To have a great day on your mission, you must overcome temptation.

One of the best ways to stay out of temptation's path is through obedience. The angel came to Adam and said, "Why dost thou offer sacrifices unto the Lord? And Adam said unto him: I know not, save the Lord commanded me" (Moses 5:6). If you compare your mission to what's going on in another mission, you'll be in trouble. Total, complete loyalty and obedience to your mission president is like unto being obedient to your Heavenly Father, for it is the law. "I, the Lord, am bound when ye do what I say" (D&C 82:10). When His servants speak, it's the same as if the Lord speaks (see D&C 1:38).

In the mission field, if you ever set yourself up as the judge, the jury, and the maker of the rules, then you will not be happy. You will not follow your president, and you'll wonder why things are not going right. So, to have a great day on your mission, do as your mission president asks, and you shall be blessed.

STUDY AND PRACTICE

One of the biggest problems in the mission field is failure to study. You have two hours every morning, from 7:30 to 9:30, to study. We often think we know enough and we don't need to do our studying.

We lose the knowledge that gives us power. We lose the preparation that precedes power. Then we become fearful because we're not well prepared. If ye are prepared ye shall not fear (see D&C 38:30). Yes, it is important to study in order to have a great day on your mission.

Elder Kramer, a great missionary, wrote me: "Dear President I had a wonderful experience this last week. It shows you that if you study hard it really pays off." He had read D&C 22:2, where it says if a man is baptized 100 times it "availeth him nothing" if it wasn't with the right authority. He continued, "One of my investigators was all ready to be baptized when he said, 'Elder Kramer, I've decided I'm not going to be baptized because I've been baptized before.' But President, then I remembered what I had studied. I asked him if he had read the Doctrine and Covenants. 'Oh yes, I love the Doctrine and Covenants,' he said. So I turned to section twenty-two and read verse two, where it asks what good it does to be baptized 100 times without the proper authority. And then the man said, 'Elder Kramer you're right, I must be baptized the right way. I'll be baptized Sunday as planned.'" Because Elder Kramer had the power and the knowledge, he had the answer. And he had studied to find that answer.

One time, when I was out teaching with the elders, I was talking to one of the investigators, and he said, "President Pinegar I want to talk to you; come with me." The elders stood there visiting in the living room, and we walked outside and he said, "I want to tell you something about your missionaries." (They weren't mine, they were the Lord's; but they were like my sons because I loved them so much.) He said, "You know what? I'm joining the Church next month, and you know one of the reasons I am?"

I said, "Well it's because you know it's true and you feel the Spirit."

He said, "Yes, but it's something about your missionaries."

I said, "What is it?"

He said, "You know President Pinegar, they always have the answer, and the way they give it to me, well, I just want to believe." Some missionaries have the power of the Spirit because they study and work hard.

So when a person says, "I don't want to hear anymore from you," maybe it's because we aren't as prepared as we should be. We must study the scriptures, our discussions, our gospel study guide, our booklets, our area book, and our investigator records; we must study and organize every needful thing so that we can preach the gospel with power and by the Spirit.

WORK

President Benson, when speaking to the mission presidents, mentioned that ninety-five percent of all the problems in the missionary field could be solved with work. Work, work, work, that's the key to success. Idleness is the den of iniquity, and every time, every single time, an elder has a problem in the mission field, is because he's idle. Idleness can and will destroy. When you grow up and have children, be sure to have them work. Just have them work. Keep them busy. I never realized how important that was until I was older. I'm thankful for my father because he taught me to work and obey. The work ethic is crucial.

One time I was out to dinner with my sweetheart, and an elder there said, "President Pinegar, our mission was right next to your mission. You know, I couldn't understand why you were having so much success there."

And I said, "Well it wasn't me, it was the missionaries and the Lord; I just happened to be there."

He said, "Well yes, but I was talking to one of your missionaries the other day and told him I couldn't understand why I wasn't more successful. And then he told me about the work ethic of your mission. And you know what? We didn't work as hard as your missionaries did."

I said, "I understand. I would actually have to say, 'Elders, please don't get up so early. Be sure to be in bed on time because you're all working too hard.'" Can you imagine the joy of that for a mission president? I actually heard the missionaries say, "President, I have the greatest schedule. I'm up at 4:30 now, I've exercised by 5:30, I've got everything done and we're out at 7:30, instead of 9:30, and I'm getting in about seventy-five hours a week." I'd look at them and just hearing them talk I'd get tired. But they were so devoted, and you know what happened? I watched on a regular basis as missionaries' bodies were renewed. The sisters, they were magnificent. The young elders, they were magnificent. The couples, oh they were just wonderful. The older single sisters were just beautiful. I can't tell you how much I loved them because I knew they were working for the Lord, and working together. It was sheer joy.

Your work ethic must be beyond reproach, but working hard is not enough. You must work smart. You must organize your time so that when you work you're effective in your work. Don't go to one area, then another, then another, in the same day. Plan your work to be in one area so you save all that travel time. Organize your time to work hard and smart. It helps you to have a happy day.

COMPANIONSHIPS

If you want to have a great day, be with your companion and build a relationship so strong that you are one. "A new commandment I give unto you, That ye love one another . . . By this shall all men know that ye are my disciples" (John 13:34–35). If you want to have a bad day, don't stay with your companion—every major problem happens when missionaries are separated. You can have a very tough day on your mission if you have companionship problems. Ask any husband or wife, when things aren't going well at home, how nice it is to be home. They will tell you that home is not such a happy place. You will have the same trouble in the mission field if you don't maintain a relationship with your companion built on trust, love, and respect.

When you get your letter from the Prophet, remember, you are a disciple of Jesus Christ, a minister of the Lord, a full-time minister—every day you are Christ's representative. What kind of missionary are you going to be? What kind of companion will you be? Will you be full of love? One who supports your companion?

Sometimes your companion doesn't want to work, your companion has a problem. What do you say? "Dear Mom and Dad, have I got a loser. The guy doesn't want to go out. This is the lamest thing. They say missionary work's the best. I can hardly stand this. This is just more than I can handle. He doesn't want to be on a mission. Why did he want to come out here? I'm out here begging him. Anyway, I can just hardly handle it." Now stop and think. Is that what we should say? If we've done it unto the least of these my brethren we've done it unto . . . ? How about this, "Heavenly Father, Elder Bill is having such a hard time today and he doesn't want to go out. Help me help him so he will want to go out. Help me tell the president in the right way so he'll inspire me to do what's right, and maybe the president can talk to him so he can be a good missionary. Heavenly Father, please just bless my companion. He just doesn't understand, and he needs help." Isn't that what a mother and father do for a child. Have you ever heard your mother and father say, "You stupid dork, why in the world were you given to me anyway?" You don't hear that. Good mothers and fathers don't say that. Do everything you can to bless and encourage your companion. And if you don't, you won't have a great day on your mission.

WATCH OVER THE FLOCK

If we read the great commandment in Matthew 22:36–40, we find that love is the fulfillment of all the law and the prophets; because in the love of God, and the love of Christ, all things are fulfilled. Now you can understand why love is the key to the entire plan of salvation.

When Jesus was talking with His disciples at the Sea of Tiberias, He said, "Peter, lovest thou me?" And Peter answered, "Yea Lord, thou know I lovest thee." In the Greek New Testament, the word *love*—the first time when used in the Aramaic or Hebrew—translates into three forms. There are three forms of *love* English just does not describe. In Greek they are *agape*, which means unconditional love; *philia*, which means brotherly and reciprocating love; and *eros*, which means physical love. So the Lord says to Peter, "Peter agape me?"

And Peter says, "Yea Lord philia."

Then the Savior tells Peter to feed His sheep. The Lord then asks again, "Peter, agape me?"

To which Peter answers, "Yea Lord, philia."

Finally, the third time, the Lord gives up and He says, "Philia me Peter?"

"Yea Lord philia."

Then the Lord instructs Peter, "Feed my sheep" (See John 21:15–17). And what the Lord was trying to say was, "Peter, do you love as God loves? Can you be unconditionally kind? Can you *act* rather than *react*? Can you avoid being vindictive, and look to be prayerful and be kind? Can you avoid contention? Can you seek the Spirit? Can you find something to praise, rather than find fault?"

Unconditional godlike love means that you have ultimate concern for every person you see in this world, and that brings about righteous service. Now think about that as it relates to Christ—ultimate concern. God loves His children. Jesus Christ loves His brothers and sisters, Heavenly Father's children. He has ultimate concern for our welfare; He died on the cross and suffered for our sins in Gethsemane, that we might live again and be resurrected if we would but repent. That's the kind of ultimate concern that brings about righteous service.

Unconditional godlike love means that I love you, and I separate you from your behavior. No matter what you do I will always love you and try to help you come unto Christ—like the Sons of Mosiah. The point is this: look for the good, look to serve, and look to be a beacon of light rather than a judge.

To be a great missionary and have a great day, you must look to serve like Christ did. You must have His ultimate, twenty-four-hours-a-day concern. You must be a full-time minister, a full-time servant, every day. You're not just to baptize and forget them. You're to be out there every day, building up the kingdom of God, strengthening members and building confidence with them. Visit those who are less active. In our mission we had a goal to visit one less-active every day. Within six months 200 members were reactivated and 400 more had come to church, just because our missionaries were full-time servants seeing less-actives as well. You don't put notches on your belt when you baptize. You don't put hash marks in your journal. No, no, no! You put the name of the child of God you were able to serve, because you're a full-time minister. You work with your priesthood leaders to receive instructions from them. You help your new converts. You continually follow up with visits, loving and nurturing your brothers and sisters.

And after they had been received unto baptism, and were wrought upon and cleansed by the power of the Holy Ghost, they were numbered among the people of the church of Christ; and their names were taken, that they might be remembered and nourished by the good word of God, to keep them in the right way, to keep them continually watchful unto prayer, relying alone upon the merits of Christ, who was the author and the finisher of their faith" (Moroni 6:4).

Think of that, when converts are baptized you keep working with them on a regular basis. And as you do this, every day will be a joyful day.

When people are committed for baptism, follow through carefully. Bridge the gap with the members. Take members with you whenever you can so there is a social connection with the investigator or new convert. Our joy is to bring souls unto Christ. This is our duty, to proclaim the gospel, to bring all Heavenly Father's children that come within the sound of our voice back home to our Heavenly Father.

Make your baptisms special—have a printed program if possible, be sure that people are notified and invited well in advance; make sure that everyone is prepared, that the ward mission leader is there, the bishop is there, and everyone is in place so that the baptism is a wonderful event. I'll never forget the day the elders said, "Oh President Pinegar, be sure and come to the baptism." I thought I could make it. I drove twenty or thirty miles down to the baptism. I got there and the building was locked. The investigator to be baptized was out front with a couple of members. The elders had forgotten to tell their ward mission leader, and the font wasn't full. It takes about an hour to fill the font. No program was printed, no program was even arranged, but the elders just had to get him baptized that afternoon no matter what. I became very sick to my stomach. I felt like I had let the Lord down. And I'll never forget when I walked in and the missionary could not even look me in the eye because he knew he'd let me down, and he'd let the Lord down, and he let the investigator down. Baptisms are so sacred and so special. To have a great day on your mission, make each baptism memorable, because they only happen once. Needless to say, those missionaries always had wonderful baptisms after that learning experience.

SERVICE

Seek to serve. Once you start thinking of yourself, that's when the problems begin. Your problems will become difficult when you become selfish in nature rather than looking to serve. So, every morning say, "Whom can I bless? How can I help my companion? Can I call anybody up to help them?" In other words, a seeking-to-serve attitude makes a difference on your mission.

One of the biggest problems in the mission field is the use of numbers. Everyone says, "Oh my zone leader, all he cares about is my numbers. Six first discussions. Five copies of the Book of Mormon. Two committed. Five second discussions, four other general discussions. All they do is call me up and say what are your numbers? And I feel like I'm just a machine out here turning in numbers." And the only reason missionaries feel that way is because they don't understand what a number means. In the field, when you think of a number, think of it this way: Six first discussions; "Dear President, this week was a joyful week. I had the blessing of teaching six special people the first discussion of the gospel of Jesus Christ. Oh, and several of them are going on with the second and third, and we've had some of those already. It was wonderful President. It's so good. Yes, six discussions."

People often separate the number from what the number stands for. Numbers in the mission field are a representation of your Christlike service to Heavenly Father's children. "Heavenly Father, today's a great day. I taught six of Thy children the first discussion. I placed two copies of the Book of Mormon with two people who promised to read it, and I feel so good." Numbers represent Christlike service, and you become validated by the Lord. You will never seek to contend with your companion or your leaders because of numbers.

AVOID CONTENTION

Contention in the mission field—back biting and gossiping—probably ruins more days than anything else. We must learn to bridle our tongue, our passions; to speak kind and loving things; and to avoid contention. Contention is of the devil (see 3 Ne. 11:28–29).

It was 10:30 at night, every missionary should be in bed. Whenever the phone rings at 10:30 at night, something's wrong. The phone rang. I answered and heard the voice of a great zone leader. "Hello President, I've got a problem. One of the couples is upset with two of the missionaries because something happened that didn't go right, and the bishop's upset now, and I'm the zone leader, and you told me to take care of it and I don't know what to do. The couple's angry at me, and the elders didn't think they were at fault, and the bishop's ready to call you up. I just don't know what to do."

I said, "Elder, pray tonight, and you call me tomorrow morning at 6:30 and we will counsel together on the things that the Lord would have you do."

Later that night the couple called. "President Pinegar, we want to see you tomorrow morning."

I said, "I have a commitment."

"No, we have to see you."

I said, "What's the matter?"

"These two elders in our ward . . . and you know . . . well they deserve . . . and we want to make sure they understand it now." That was the basic tone of the conversation. Everyone was upset.

The next morning the zone leader called, and contention was still rampant. The zone leader asked, "President, what shall I do?"

I said, "Elder, first have a kneeling prayer, then read them Moroni 7:44–48; John 13:34–35 and Matthew 25:40. Then suggest in the spirit of love and charity, 'Let us solve our problem so we can be happy in the service of the Lord.'" That was more or less the instruction. Two hours later the phone rang. "President, I just had the greatest day of my life. President, you never grow until you have a challenge. I was just sick to my stomach, but the Spirit of the Lord was so strong. We all cried, we all hugged, we all loved each other. We're going to do it. We made up. Things are right, and President, the Lord healed us. The Lord healed us."

Yes, to have a great day on our mission, we do our best and the Spirit will guide and direct us. We'll have no regrets. Put it on your refrigerator. I heard Bishop Hales speak at the MTC once, and he said, "Return with Honor." So then I encouraged them to "Return with honor with no regrets." The main thing is to do your best. Sometimes at the MTC the elders might not have been at their perfect best. People would say, "President Pinegar, do you know what the elders did?" And I would say, "Do you mean some of the Lord's anointed weren't perfect yesterday?" And they kind of bowed their heads and walked out the door because they didn't understand that sometimes we're not at our best. Forgiveness then became the watchword. And all of a sudden, doing our best was doing our best to forgive and to forget and to move forward. Yes, the days will be hard. You might say, "How can you say it was so good when it was so hard?" Every day can be fulfilling.

If you are going to have a great day on your mission, you've got to remember the words of Mormon to his son Moroni: "Notwithstanding their hardness (the investigators or the difficult situations), let us labor diligently; for if we should cease to labor, we should be brought under condemnation; for we have a labor to perform whilst in this tabernacle of clay, that we may conquer the enemy of all righteousness, and rest our souls in the kingdom of God" (Moroni 9:6).

KEEP A SENSE OF HUMOR

It's OK to laugh. Keep a sense of humor so that things won't get too tough. A cheerful and light-hearted attitude goes a long way towards making a mission more enjoyable. Cheerfulness and a sense of humor are some of the most uplifting and contagious attributes one can possess. They brighten both the giver and those who choose to receive it. They give hope for the day ahead and even enhance physiological and emotional health. Cheerfulness and good humor come from seeing that we are all in the same boat. Laugh at yourself and laugh with others. Be cheerful despite life's adversities—it's a welcome commandment of God (see John 16:33; D&C 123:17), and it makes life flow more smoothly. The Psalmist said, "Serve the Lord with gladness" (Psalm 100:2). Make the decision to be cheerful. Make it a point to keep a sense of humor. Why are some people so spontaneously cheerful? Because they *choose* to be. And so can you.

CONCLUSION

And whatever you do, write home to Mom and Dad, and that special friend, because you know what? To have a great day on a mission is to share it with others. Everyone loves letters from a missionary. They're beautiful. In our mission, when I was mission president, several parents were baptized through letters from their missionary children. Many parents were reactivated through letters from their daughters and their sons; and grandchildren reactivated through their grandparents. You want to have a great day? Be a missionary every day of your life. You'll never know when the Lord will speak to you and tell you to do something. You are a missionary every day of your life, so you can have a great day every day of your life.

That's the kind of day you can have on your mission—a great day. Whether a member missionary, or a full-time missionary. The joy becomes great when we help Heavenly Father's children. All that matters is today. The past is gone, the future is not yet here. Do you want to have a great day? Then do the will of the Father, and every day will be a great day in your life.

☞ CHAPTER 6 ☜

BEING CONTINUALLY MOTIVATED AS A MISSIONARY

When I worked on the Church Missionary Training Committee, I would train mission presidents during the mission presidents' seminar. In preparation for that training, I surveyed mission presidents already out on assignment and asked them what their main responsibility was. "Motivating missionaries is ninety-five percent of my work," they almost always replied. "Missionaries get discouraged, they get tired, they get worn out." One of the most difficult things we face as missionaries is staying motivated. This seems to be the challenge throughout every mission in all the world. Missionaries have good days and struggling days. We have successes and trials. Sometimes in our work we lose the power that is within us because we lose the vision, or fail to appreciate the Atonement and look to Christ for our strength. We can be continually motivated and successful missionaries if our perception is clear and our motives pure.

CONVERSION

There are many reasons why we do what we do as missionaries. Most of the time there are variety of reasons all acting at once. We grow and progress spiritually as our motives change. Sometimes missionaries would say to me, "I came just because all my brothers went; what else could I do? They would think I'd done something wrong if I didn't come."

I would say, "I'm just grateful that you're here, and I love you and I know the Lord loves you." Those same elders, weeks, or months, or maybe even a year later, would be in an interview and I would notice a glowing countenance. I would ask, "How do you feel about your mission now?"

And I would hear: "Oh President, I love the Jones family so much, I'm just praying that they'll come back into the Church," or, "I love the Brown family; I think they're ready to be committed to be baptized. Oh I just pray that the Lord will be pleased with what I'm doing. I just want to do what He would have me do if He were here." Motives change because our relationship to Christ, and our understanding and appreciation of the doctrines, principles, and covenants have caused a change within us so that we do things for the right reasons, rather than just because we're told to do them.

Sometimes we are motivated by love, duty, responsibility, peer or parental pressure, a desire for self-improvement, power or self-esteem. Still, other sources of motivation come from our need or desire for success, respect, the love and trust of our leaders, a new value system, and joy. We can also be motivated by the vision of possibilities and the traditions of righteousness. And there is merit in all these motives. But our Heavenly Father, our Savior Jesus Christ, and the Holy Ghost, are the supreme sources of motivation. The plan of our Heavenly Father, when understood, should give us all we need. If we are rooted in Jesus Christ, listen to the living prophets, and adhere to the scriptures, we will have a continual living well of motivation. We love God and our fellowmen and that's why we should do what we do. It has been said that no one motivates us; rather, we are given information that we act upon, then we choose to be motivated.

We can choose to be motivated when we understand the significance of the following questions: (1) Do we know our purpose? (2) Why are we truly here? (3) Do we recognize the worth of souls? (4) Do we understand the purpose of the Church? (5) Do we want all of our brothers and sisters to have a chance for happiness and exaltation? (6) And above all, do we comprehend the significance of the Atonement of Jesus Christ?

Many of the personal attributes we have already discussed will help us stay motivated as well: desire from within; the vision of the work; humility, which allows us to learn and submit to the will of our Father; positive attitude, which gives us hope that we're willing to press forward and to work with all our heart; and being able to make and keep commitments and live a disciplined life. These attributes of success can help us stay motivated in the Lord's work.

We grow spiritually as we fast and pray, search the scriptures, and keep the commandments of the Lord. We want to cultivate charity, for when we have charity we will be like the Lord. We will live the doctrine of Christ through faith, repentance, making the covenant of baptism, and being given the gift of the Holy Ghost. These are practices that will help us stay motivated. But most important of all, we must be built upon the rock of the Lord Jesus Christ. Are we converted to Jesus Christ? Our behavior is nothing more than a reflection of the depth of our conversion to Jesus Christ. The deeper the conversion, the greater the motivation and the greater the Christlike behavior.

Here are some things that will help us in our conversion to Christ: (1) Do we have a knowledge of the character of our Heavenly Father and His plan, and His Only Begotten Son, our Savior Jesus Christ? (2) Do we have a relationship with our Heavenly Father and our Savior based on the three great firsts: faith, love, and obedience? (3) Do we continually recognize our dependence on our Heavenly Father? (4) And do we understand the reason for Heavenly Father's actions towards us? When we come to understand some of these things, we will be truly motivated—yes, even self-motivated.

We must also have increased desire to serve the Lord. How do we get this desire? When our faith increases, our love increases. We can understand our purpose. When we realize that we've been forgiven of our sins, we can taste the joy of the Lord. Alma, after his conversion, says that his joy was to preach these words (see Alma 36:24). He wanted everyone to taste of the joy he had tasted. Do you think Alma's desire was strong? Of course it was. Whenever we have any success our desire will increase proportionately.

How do we keep our vision strong and the purpose of the work in our minds and hearts? It's when we realize the purpose of God's plan, and God's plan for us as missionaries. We become instruments through which Heavenly Father and Jesus Christ's purposes are fulfilled. We can do all things the Lord has asked us to do because we are His disciples. We are like Mormon when he said, "Behold I am a disciple of Jesus Christ . . . I have been called of him to declare his word . . . that [people] might have everlasting life" (3 Ne. 5:13). In other words, when we catch the vision and understand His purposes, our motivation should increase.

When we are easily entreated it's easier to stay motivated. If we are always asking, "How come we have to do ten of those and five of these? why are we working so hard? why are zone meetings on this day instead of that day? why are we doing this?" then we are not easy to entreat. If we choose to always backbite and complain, we will not be easily entreated, and we will not stay motivated.

If you're rooted to Christ you can stay motivated. When another door slams, you'll say, "Great, let the door slam. That will really give me a blessing you know. Throw water on me, anything. I need the blessings." And if you have that kind of positive attitude, you'll be marvelous.

AN ATTITUDE OF ENTHUSIASM

Maintaining a positive attitude is the magic key to motivation. You can be no better than your attitude, because attitude is part of your perception. Perception comes through your past experience, your values, and your attitude. I recall the story I once told to a group of people about a little girl in the fifth grade. It is picture day at school and she is so excited. Her mother says, "Let's put on your white dress; it's such a beautiful March spring day. The snow is almost melted. You will look so pretty in your white dress for the school picture." Once she is dressed in her finery, the little girl runs up quickly to the bus stop and she's first in line. Along comes a car, and splot, splat—mud all over her dress; oh it was horrible. She runs back home crying, "Mommy, Mommy, my dress is ruined, my dress is ruined."

Then she goes in the house and her mother says, "Well let's put on your second-best dress." So she puts on her second-best dress and she runs back to the bus stop. Just as she gets to the bus stop she reaches up to grab the bus handle, but the bus driver didn't see her and he inadvertently closes the door and hits her right on the nose—boom. Hemoglobin is everywhere. She takes her little hanky and tries to stop her nosebleed. She finally gets to school. She has a little scabby nose, but she has her second-best dress on, so it's not too bad of a day. Well, she goes to morning recess on the north side of the building. There are a few little parcels of snow still left, and some young, future missionary boys in the fifth grade are making snowballs. They decide to throw one that goes the wrong way, and lo and behold, it hits her right in the eye—kaboom! Her eye begins to swell up, and she runs to the teacher. "Teacher, teacher, look at my eye."

"Yes, it's swollen shut. Well Sweety Pie, you go on the south side of the building for recess next time. It's warm there and those snowballs won't hit you anymore."

"OK teacher, I will." Next recess, in the afternoon, she climbs up on the tricky bars (the monkey bars), all the way to the top. There she is sitting at the top when she sees her friend Sally. She goes to wave and loses her grip and—khkh khkh khkh—falls all the way down and lands on her elbow. She screams, but as she screams, she notices something shiny on the ground and clutches it in her hand. She cries her way into the teacher and says, "My arm hurts." The teacher thinks, "Oh dear, it's probably broken." Then the school nurse comes and agrees that the arm is probably broken. "Let's put it in a sling and call her mother so she can take her to the doctor." So, they put the arm in the sling and her mother comes to pick her up. And there's her daughter, swollen eye, scabby nose, second-best dress on, sling on her arm, and a smile on her face. And she says, "Sweetheart, how can you smile on a day like this?"

And the little girl says, "Oh Mommy, it was my lucky day—I found a nickel." Now that's what I call a positive attitude.

There are going to be days you get all the doors slammed, but to stay motivated, your attitude must be positive. "Blessed are all they who are persecuted for my name's sake" (3 Ne. 12:10). So every time you're persecuted you're getting a blessing. The next time you go down the street, and no one lets you in, and people say unkind things, you are getting blessings. That's the kind of attitude we have to have. It doesn't matter where we are; that positive attitude can save lives, because if we always feel good about ourselves and the work, then we'll keep plugging along.

In our mission we had an attitude of "always one more door." So we would knock on all the doors and one more. Well, one day we were having a zone meeting and one of the sisters stood up to speak. The sister said, "Oh President, it was a hard day. It was raining and we'd forgotten our brawleys (that's umbrellas in England). Things weren't going well, and all I could remember you saying was 'one more door, one more door.' We were now sopping wet and you know what? I could just hear that little voice of yours, President, saying 'one more door, one more door.' I felt so good inside, and I kept saying, 'I've got a good attitude and I'm sopping wet, and I don't care.' And then we knocked on that one more door and this lady looked at us like, 'You poor little wet things, you'll turn into a fish if you stay out much longer.' And sure enough she invited us in and we gave a first discussion."

You must recognize the purpose of opposition in all things. It's here to stay. You must needs be tempted to know the good from the evil. You have opposition so you can grow, and you have the right to choose. You have moral agency, which is a gift from God. You can decide when you wake up in the morning—it's a great day or it's not. You are the decision maker. Realize that you have the power to choose to *react* or to *act*. If your attitude is one of doubt, guess what just left your very being—faith. For where doubt dwells, faith cannot exist. Yes, when we draw on the powers of heaven, and strengthen our spirituality through prayer and study and personal righteousness, we will gain confidence and our attitude will be positive.

Make reachable, measurable goals, with logical and systematic plans. Implement the plans by the Spirit with dates of accomplishment to do your work. And when you do that, you'll start to have a little more success. Success begets success, and then you'll want to keep working hard because you are motivated.

REALIZING YOUR DIVINE POTENTIAL

If I could talk to you like you were just sitting right next to me, one on one, I would tell you that you are fulfillment of prophecy. As in Jacob 5:70–71, you are the one who is pruning the vineyard for the last time. You are among those of whom the Lord spoke in the D&C 138:53–57. He talks about the temple and proclaiming the gospel to the vineyard again. Yes, you are one of the noble and great ones saved for this day. Don't you realize how special you are? Because when you realize how special you are, you will keep working. Realize that because of your exceeding good works in the premortal existence, you are now here doing that great work of bringing souls unto Christ by building up the kingdom of God (see Alma 13:3–7). So I praise you; I honor you. You are held in high esteem. You must be instructed in the ways of the Lord at your zone meetings, at your district meetings, and from your beloved president who loves you with all of his heart. And then remember, you can do it. There's nothing you cannot do.

The Lord motivates us. He motivates us because He has our respect. We trust Him and we love Him, and He blesses our lives. He motivates us because we recognize our weaknesses and imperfections and trust Him to give us the help we need. He motivates us by showing us our divine potential. "You are my sons, you are my daughters, you can come and be with me." He motivates us by giving us a new value system, the plan of exaltation, the plan of happiness. And, He motivates us by requiring us to make and keep commitments that He calls covenants. As your commitment to your covenants deepens, your motivation increases. Remember that God has covenanted with us to give us all things. Is this not motivation enough: exaltation and happiness?

We can be motivated in all things, but the key comes down to this: how converted are we to Christ and His gospel? How deep is our gratitude for His atoning sacrifice? Then you can be like the missionary who stood up and said, "It's the least I could do to be a good missionary after all my Savior has done for me."

Bringing souls to Christ is the goal and the reward. Nothing could make us happier. A missionary I taught in missionary preparation class just wrote me. He's serving in Germany. He wrote, "Oh Brother Ed, it's so great. A sister is committed for February 8 to be baptized. It's like you said, I've never been so happy." And then he said some beautiful words, "I am continually being strengthened by the Atonement of the Lord Jesus Christ. There are elders and sisters who understand why we do what we do. And when we think of a baptismal goal, or any other worthy goals, it's because we love Heavenly Father's children." Surely this love will be our motive in missionary work. Love is the motive for Heavenly Father and our Savior in all that they do (see John 3:16; 2 Ne. 26:24).

CONCLUSION

You will become successful by having faith in Christ, by having the love of Christ, and obeying all of Christ's commandments, and then the Spirit will be yours and you will be strong. You will be continually motivated and successful as a missionary for the Lord Jesus Christ.

⇥ 𝒞HAPTER 7 ⇤

COMMUNICATING

Until we learn to communicate, no one will know our hearts, no one will know the love we have for them, and no one will know us. Communication is the key to building relationships of trust. A strong relationship is vital to both the receiving and giving of the blessings of the gospel.

COMMUNICATING WITH GOD

To communicate with others, we must first learn to communicate with the Father who gave us life; learning to communicate with our Heavenly Father becomes the foundation for all our communications.

We usually call this communication prayer; we might even say mighty prayer. In John the Beloved's gospel he said, "And this is life eternal, that they might know thee the only true God, and Jesus Christ, whom thou hast sent" (John 17:3). Knowing God is an essential element of communication. The Prophet Joseph Smith said that before you can have faith in God, you must know Him and know His character (see *Lectures on Faith* 4:1). Those of you who have had the privilege of reading the *Lectures on Faith* know whereof I speak, for the first lecture is all about the character and nature of God. Now that's interesting, because if you look closely at your first discussion, you will see it teaches that God is our Father, that He knows all, and that He is all loving and all powerful. So, when we teach that discussion, we plant the seeds of desire to know our Heavenly Father.

KNOWING OUR FATHER

In section 67 of the Doctrine and Covenants, the Prophet received a revelation in Hyrum, Ohio, about knowing God. Verse 10 is especially beautiful because it relates specifically to missionaries:

> And again, verily I say unto you that it is your privilege, and a promise I give unto you that have been ordained unto this ministry, that inasmuch as you strip yourselves from jealousies [which are very bad] and fears [which are not very good], and humble yourselves before me, for ye are not sufficiently humble, the veil shall be rent and you shall see me and know that I am— not with the carnal neither natural mind, but with the spiritual.

In other words, we can never know our Father until we overcome jealousies and fears, and humble ourselves.

Overcome Jealousy with Love

What would you say is the absolute antithesis, or opposite, of jealousy? It is love and charity, because jealousy cannot coexist with those feelings. If you find yourself feeling jealous of other people's intellect, their looks, their clothes, or their possessions, you know that in your heart you lack the love of God, and the love of Christ—even charity. It will be like a barometer. When you see somebody doing something good or doing something better than you, maybe looking better or wearing a nicer suit, you say, "Isn't that nice! Isn't that beautiful! Boy, he did well on that, didn't he!" Just watch yourself grow. You see, in the hereafter nobody is going to ask you what car you drove, or how big your house was, or what kind of hair you had (or, in my case, didn't have).

Look for opportunities to praise people rather than tear them down. When you tear others down, you go down with them. You dig your own pit. When you build people up, you rise with them. Jealousy can be destroyed through the power of love.

Five Ways to Overcome Fear

We overcome fear with faith, love, preparation, knowledge, and experience. Fear is a destroyer of faith. Our prayers cannot be with real intent when we are suffering from fear.

Learn Humility

The last step is humility. Until we humble ourselves, there will be no spiritual growth. It's interesting to note that in Helaman 3:35, the Nephites did fast and pray oft, waxing stronger and stronger in their humility. If you want to be strong in humility, pray with real intent and you'll have that humility. By exercising humility, love, faith, and knowledge—combined with mighty prayer—we will learn to know our Father.

COMMUNICATING WITH YOUR COMPANION

There are three major areas to work on when communicating with your companion: expressing your love, building trust, and using the words of the Spirit.

Express Your Love

We must understand that everybody really wants to be loved, and the people who seem the most cocky are often the ones who are most in need of love. Take the time to get down on the root level with your companion and district leader and show love.

I had some glorious experiences with the youth in our stake when we went on a pioneer trek. We divided up into "families." There was simply no one else for us to talk to but each other. All of a sudden we were all forced to learn the process of communicating.

After three days in the wilderness, a testimony meeting was held. I'll never forget one boy who thought he was pretty cool. He stood up and said, "I was with old Jason in our ward. I always thought that Jason was such a nerd, I wouldn't have given him the time of day. But let me tell you, Jason was in our family on this trek, and I got to know him, and now I love Jason. He is my dear pal, and we'll be friends forever. Oh, I love that guy! I wish I had taken the time before this to become his pal."

You can save yourselves a lot of problems during this earth life by expressing the love of God and the love of Christ through communication. Whether it be verbal, by touch, or by whatever means, please communicate your love (see John 13:34–35). I know it takes time and it takes effort, but nothing else you do during your mission will bring greater rewards. And without communicating your love, true communication simply won't occur.

Of course you won't meet your companion and immediately say, "Oh, you're my companion, and I love you!" That doesn't happen. Neither does "Oh, we're married in the temple. Great! That's it for eternal life—super!" It's like the man who said to his wife, when she was feeling unloved and unappreciated, "I told you that I loved you and that if it ever changed I'd let you know. So why are you so upset?" We all need more than that. Even I need to be told every day that I'm loved.

When my daughter Tricia was a young girl she'd wait for me to get home every night. When I'd come in the door she would greet me with, "Hi, Daddy, I love ya!" My heart warmed, I smiled, and my burdens were lifted.

In your communication, start the process now of working with yourself and with your companion and learning to express your love for each other and the great work that you are doing together.

Build Trust and Prepare to Accept Loving Feedback

In communication, one of the most difficult things to deal with is when we are doing something that may not be perfect, and we need counsel on it, and everyone else can see it except us. Let me tell you how it started in our family.

"Sweetheart," my wife said to me one day, "I think we need to take time to evaluate each other and how we're doing." So we had our first big evaluation (we call it companionship inventory). We sat down and I said, "Honey, how are you doing? How am I doing? What could I work on?"

"Oh you're fine, sweetheart," she answered. "But it might be nice if you'd work a little more in the yard."

"What do you mean?" I bristled. *I've been slaving away in mouths (I'm a dentist), filling cavities, taking out wisdom teeth—foraging in the field for food—and you're worried about whether or not I'm working in the yard!?* I didn't say that, but I thought that!

I simply wasn't ready to accept any constructive criticism. Feedback requires a person to say, "Tell me what I can change; I am ready and open and willing to listen." It almost takes the courage of David because our hearts are so very sensitive and vulnerable. What you have to do is establish trust in your relationship first. Once you build a relationship of trust, then you can communicate and say, "Help me." And when you do that in your companionship, you will really begin to grow.

My wife can tell me anything now, and I'm so grateful because we have a relationship in which I can say, "Sweetheart . . . ." and she understands what I'm trying to communicate.

The other day I was having a tough day, feeling a little sick and weak and powerless. I came into the house, found my darling wife, and said, "Sweetheart . . ." I was totally exhausted and I wanted to go to sleep, yet I knew I couldn't. She saw that, heard the plea in my voice, and gave me a hug.

"Honey, I just need some strength," I said. "I'm getting weak." I felt her strength in that hug pouring into me, sustaining me, and carrying me through the rest of the day. She understood my troubles, and loved and supported me with the love of Christ. She didn't say, "Why don't you do this?" or "Why don't you do that?" She didn't find fault with me or scold my weakness. She simply loved me because we share a deep trust in our relationship.

We will never be able to give productive feedback until we build a relationship of trust. After we have reached that level, then we can be open and candid, and say, "Help me, Elder, or Sister, what do I really need?"

It's so wonderful now when my wife says, "Sweetheart, it would really help if you would . . . ." And I can answer, "Oh honey, thank you, I'll be so much better." Feedback is the essence of humility.

After we have a relationship of trust in our communication, we have enough humility to say, "OK, tell me because I want to grow." If we have an insatiable desire to be like the Savior, people can say, "Hey, you've got to change that, you need to shape up." And we'll be able to answer, "OK, OK, I'll be better." As missionaries, when you can do that, you will change, and the communication in your companionship will be open, candid, and honest.

Use the Spirit's Words, Not the World's

We can only communicate honestly if we are led by the Spirit—in other words, when we ask ourselves in every situation, "What would Jesus do?" and "How would the Spirit direct us?" If any of you were to say "President, I need to see you" and then come in for an interview, long before you ever walked in the door, I would have already prayed: "Father, what would you have me say by the Spirit if Thou were here at this very moment?"

If our communication is honest and open, it will always be led by the Spirit, and that is vital in preventing hurt feelings. Communication should never be intended to harm anyone. Yet, so often our communication is flippant, light-minded, casual, and worldly. It seems that everything now has to be fun or funny. I'm not saying we can't laugh (I love to laugh as much as anyone else), but there's a right time and a right place.

Sober-mindedness is one of the most essential traits in order to be a spiritual giant, in order to speak by the Spirit, to be led by the Spirit, to be Ammon-like and Moroni-like missionaries. The language we use is an important key in maintaining sober-mindedness. Words like "He's a cool dude" are totally inappropriate. Phrases like "Hey, what a studman" are also totally inappropriate. That's the way the world talks, not the way the Lord would have His missionaries talk. We need to communicate the way the Spirit communicates—with love, tenderness, and sensitivity, as well as appropriately. When we don't communicate properly we often offend and hurt others.

Do you know what it means when the scriptures tell us to say "yea, yea" and "nay, nay" (see Matt. 5:37)? It means that our integrity is so strong, that whatever we say is the final word on the matter and people can absolutely trust us. When we say yes, people will know that the answer is yes and we won't have to take an oath. Our communication needs to be totally honest, straightforward, on a higher plane than the rest of the world because we are disciples of Christ.

COMMUNICATING WITH INVESTIGATORS

There are many things we should do with investigators to build relationships of trust and help them feel the Spirit. Some of them are as easy as smiling, and some require our own spiritual fine-tuning.

Just Smile

I'd like to move into the aspect of communication during your initial contact with an investigator. We've talked about the principles of knowing our Heavenly Father and working with each other. Now that we're building these relationships of trust, what is the most important thing we can do every time we come in contact with another human being? Smile! What does a smile say? A smile communicates that we bear a message of happiness and friendliness. When we meet an investigator we are sharing a message so powerful, heartening, and important that we must smile! Of course, that doesn't mean we have to do it every minute, but we should make sure our first communication is accompanied by a smile.

Positive Labeling

We must also get to know the person we're communicating with. We've got to smile and say something like, "It is so nice to see you." Then follow that up with a genuine "How are you doing?" Next, we start a gospel conversation. This is one of the most important things you will learn to do on your mission: start a gospel conversation.

When you meet a person at the grocery store, or knock on someone's door, or even just see someone on the street, make it a habit to approach them and say, "Excuse me, would you be so kind and friendly as to help me in regards to a few questions that might be a blessing to your life?" Do you know what they do? They think, "Oh, I'm kind and friendly! Oh, you need help?" Do you see it? If you label a person and say, "You are kind and friendly," they act that way.

We have to be careful that we don't manipulate when we label people. If we communicate to manipulate we will be hollow and mechanical, and people will see right through us. If we're honest and we just keep loving people, and loving people, and loving people, and talking to them and giving them positive feedback, then they will listen and love us in return.

It's important that we raise the level of esteem of the person we're communicating with. Let me give you an example. I was a substitute as a basketball player during high school. I knew I was good, but the coach just didn't think I was good enough. My senior year, however, we got a new coach, and he said, "Ed, you will be my center and my captain."

Ta-dahh! He labeled me. He communicated to me and labeled me with a positive label. Guess what happened? Ed Pinegar led the region in scoring, was All-State, and selected to be on the All-Star Shrine team for the state of Utah. Why? Because a coach believed in me and communicated that to me with a positive label.

Radiating Love

Now, you senior couples will witness some of the most beautiful things you've ever seen in your lives, and all because of your capacity to love. There will be less-active members who have been less active for five or ten years, and something like this will happen when senior couples are working for the Lord. You will knock on a door and introduce yourself, "Hello Mr. Jones, we're Brother and Sister Woodbury. We have just come here on our mission, and we would love to drop in and see you. You are members of the Church?"

"Yeah, well, we don't go anymore."

"Oh, could we just come in and visit with you for a minute, just to let you know how things are?"

"Sure, come on in."

Then you share your experience with the bishop, who says, "How'd you get into that house? There hasn't been anybody in that house for ten years." You are a valuable asset to any mission president.

Couples have the maturity of life and the capacity to love because they've had us as their children. They have the power of love that radiates from their entire beings. When this love is in you, it radiates from you too. The words I've used in these sample opening conversations are fine, but if love isn't there, the words won't do anything. You see, when we really have that love, the people we meet will feel it. If we don't have it, we can pray for it with all our heart until we receive it (see Moroni 7:48). Then, when we approach others with love, our message will be communicated.

But beware! If we understand these principles and say, "Oh, I love everybody," yet live a hermit's life, it's like being a monk and saying, "Oh yes, I'm anxious to spread the gospel." Do you see the problem? Love isn't love until you give it away! Communication becomes the essence of your power to influence and strengthen others. "Therefore, strengthen your brethren in all your conversation, in all your prayers, in all your exhortations, and in all your doings" (D&C 108:7).

The Love of the Father Helps Us Communicate

When we communicate with our Father, we know how He feels, and through that communication, we also discover how we should feel. If you were to describe Heavenly Father's greatest feeling, what would it be? Love. That's the great motive in His eternal plan. And how is that feeling manifest? Where does it fit in the grand plan our Father has outlined? In His love for His children.

John 3:16 describes the great love our Heavenly Father and the Savior have for us: "For God so loved the world, that He gave his only begotten Son, that whosoever believeth in him should not perish, but have everlasting life."

In other words, when you truly love, you empathize and feel for other people. The love that God the Father, Elohim, gave to us was His Son. Christ's love for us is explained clearly in 2 Nephi 26:24:

> He doeth not anything save it be for the benefit of the world; for he loveth the world, even that he layeth down his own life that he may draw all men unto him. Wherefore, he commandeth none that they shall not partake of his salvation.

He gave His life for us; He atoned. So love, then, should emulate this feeling, this empathy toward one another.

Now, if we pray to our Heavenly Father, do we know what we seek in our communication with Him? Think about it; don't answer yet. What are you seeking when you pray to Heavenly Father? If you were to seek any kind of knowledge, or anything else for that matter, what would you seek? Hopefully, you would seek the Spirit.

What would the Spirit tell you? Think of the Savior in the garden and His submission to the will of the Father. Our insatiable desire should be the same—to do the will of the Father. And what is the will of the Father? The scriptures teach that the thing of greatest worth to our Father is the worth of the soul (see D&C 18:10). Thus we can deduce that the will of the Father is simple: that all mankind might be taught the gospel of His Son and have an opportunity to be baptized and come into His Church.

Now that we understand communication with the Father we're moving to the next level. When we seek first to understand, then we will be more easily understood. When we understand, we can more easily empathize. Empathy simply means feeling how other people feel. When we empathize, we know we are communicating. If we haven't done that yet, then we haven't communicated, and we may just have a verbal barrage going back and forth. Remember, seek first to understand, then to be understood, and finally to feel how others feel. Then we will be communicating.

So in communication we want to listen with our ears and our hearts so we can know and understand. Think of your own life when you've had a tough day. You felt misunderstood and unloved, didn't you? We've all had days like that. It really helps to have someone understand the way we feel.

Communication, then, becomes a most important tool we can use on this earth to bring happiness—both to ourselves and to others. If we don't communicate our message, our message is not heard. You should be prepared to communicate.

Make Communication Bless Lives

One thing we can do to help other people is to use our personal influence; and our personal influence is directly proportional to our ability to radiate the love of God that is within our very being.

It doesn't take a mommy or a daddy very long to learn that what they are is what they teach their children. We may use a thousand words, but it's our actions that teach our children. By the same token, what we are is what teaches our investigators, so we need to understand and build our ability to communicate in order to let the love come through.

When we love a person enough, we'll communicate according to their needs. Let me give you an example. I taught seminary for five years when I was a dental student and before I went to work as a dentist. I was teaching the New Testament, and I always had my students fill out a little form with their likes, dislikes, hobbies, etc. A young man in one of these classes always sat off to the side. Now, I wanted him to know that someone loved him, and that he felt enough of a connection to me that he'd be willing to listen to what I taught him about the gospel.

"How are you doing, Mike?" I always asked.

The reply was always the same: "OK, I guess."

Mike was simply shy. I decided I had better review his information sheet. I wondered what he really liked. *(1) Favorite class in school?* "None." *(2) Favorite book?* "None." *(3) Favorite hobbies?* "None." *(4) Favorite TV show?* "Hogan's Heros." OK, here was something at least.

That night I watched *Hogan's Heroes*. The next day Mike came into class and sat down. "Hey, Mike, what did you think of old Shultz?" I asked. "Was that a crackup last night or what?"

"Oh, Brother Ed, you mean you watch *Hogan's Heroes*?" He replied. "Hey, Brother Ed, you're OK. You like what I like."

At that point, my communication with Mike was centered on a common interest. Now, this doesn't mean we should talk about bad things with others in order to establish a common denominator; this just means we take enough time to care about people and the things they care about. And if we do that, we'll build a relationship of trust—and be able to bless their lives.

No one cares how much we know until they know how much we care. If I wanted to really communicate with anybody, I would ask myself five questions. (Keep in mind that we're communicating with people to bring them to Christ. We're trying to communicate in a way that helps us to become spiritually stronger and closer to our Savior and to our Heavenly Father.) (1) Do they know that I really care? (2) Do I really know how they feel or what they are thinking? (When I really knew how Mike felt about *Hogan's Heroes* it made a difference.) (3) Is there anything in the scriptures or in the discussions, or particularly in the Book of Mormon, that I could use to touch their heart? (4) Have they felt the Spirit, and were they aware of it? In other words, did they feel the Spirit in our communication?

After I've asked those four questions, I would ask the big one: (5) Have I invited them to do anything about it? That's the thing: we communicate to bless people's lives. Of course, we know we can casually communicate and never build up anything but verbiage. Communication that counts is communication that blesses people's lives. Those five questions, when used to evaluate our communication, will help us tremendously.

The Spirit Is the Strongest Tool

After learning these keys to communication, the tool that will make all communication effective, both during your mission and in the future, is the help of the Spirit.

In Doctrine and Covenants 50, it states that the Spirit is a converter and a teacher; the Spirit is also a communicator. A great example of the power of the Spirit is recorded in 2 Nephi, "I, Nephi, cannot write all the things which were taught among my people; neither am I mighty in writing, like unto speaking; for when a man speaketh by the power of the Holy Ghost the power of the Holy Ghost carrieth it unto the hearts of the children of men" (33:1).

This is what can happen as we work on effective communication and allow the Lord to help us:

> Neither take ye thought beforehand what ye shall say; but treasure up in your minds continually the words of life, and it shall be given you in the very hour that portion that shall be meted unto every man.
>
> Therefore, let no man among you, for this commandment is unto all the faithful who are called of God in the church unto the ministry, from this hour take purse or scrip, that goeth forth to proclaim this gospel of the kingdom.
>
> Behold, I send you out to reprove the world of all their unrighteous deeds, and to teach them of a judgment which is to come.
>
> And whoso receiveth you, there I will be also, for I will go before your face. I will be on your right hand and on your left, and my Spirit shall be in your hearts, and mine angels round about you, to bear you up (D&C 84:85–88).

As we attempt to communicate, teach, and preach, the Spirit does most of the work (see D&C 100: 5–6).

Do you see why we pray for hearts to be softened? Do you understand why, when we're humble, we can communicate? The only way that we ever reach the point of getting down to the most basic level is when heart speaks to heart through and by the Spirit.

LOVE YOURSELF WITH THE LOVE OF CHRIST

It's very difficult to love anyone else when we don't love ourselves. When you go home, look in your mirror and remind yourself of who you are. Then tell yourself that you love you because you love everyone God gave life to. Then get down on your knees and thank Heavenly Father for your life, ask for forgiveness for your weaknesses, and ask for strength to love the people you meet. Remember: you need to love yourself first.

I want you to know that I love Ed Pinegar because I'm Heavenly Father's boy. I love you, too, and I want you to be so good that you'll want to help everybody, and you'll never be unkind or make a snide remark. I never want you to do anything to hurt anybody. I hope all you want to do is communicate the love of Christ to everyone. When you're in contact with your investigators they've got to know who you are and what you stand for.

CONCLUSION

When we learn to love and care so much for our brothers and sisters that we'd do anything so that they might not endure endless torment, we will gladly pay the price to learn to communicate—with love, knowledge, and faith. Nevertheless, it can be tough. There will be times when you want to walk away, when you want to say, "I don't care." That's the biggest mistake of all! I hope you understand that as we grow in the gospel, as we gain a greater desire to show and give love, we must become great communicators by and through the Spirit. When the Spirit comes upon us, we will communicate appropriately.

I pray that we care enough to pay the price to communicate in love, thereby becoming great disciples of the Lord Jesus Christ. I know what we are doing is the Lord's will. I know it is important. I know the transcending events of our lives are when we communicate with people to bless them. I would hope that we would often get on our knees and pray to our Father. Ponder with your companion; maybe tonight will be the first night you can say, "Hey, I feel like I'm brave enough. Open up, give me just a little feedback. Not too much. Just enough to . . . well, first of all, why don't you tell me about something I'm doing well?"

"OK, I like the way you smile."

"That's good; I'll smile a little more."

Take the time to tenderly, lovingly help each other. If you're feeling especially brave, you might try to write five things that are neat about your companion. "I like you because you are bald." Or, "I like you because you've got a high, raspy voice." (Those were some reasons that my companion liked me.) Just give each other five reasons why you like each other. Post those lists above your beds, or right by the mirror, or wherever you want, and then look at them.

The next day, write three or four things that could possibly use improvement. "Maybe here's something you might, maybe possibly, perhaps if convenient, you might, you know, maybe, uh, tract." And who knows? You might help somebody. Love each other enough to help each other, but love each other enough not to destroy each other. Don't hurt anybody; this is a tender time, but it can be a growing time.

CHAPTER 8

OPENING YOUR MOUTH

One of the most important things we have to do as missionaries is to open our mouths. There is no other way we can find Heavenly Father's children. The Spirit of the Lord will give us the words we need to say. Our duty as missionaries is to invite all people to come unto Christ; everyone has a right to come unto Christ.

> Verily, verily, I say unto you, that the field is white already to harvest; wherefore, thrust in your sickles, and reap with all your might, mind, and strength. Open your mouths and they shall be filled, and you shall become even as Nephi of old, who journeyed from Jerusalem in the wilderness. Yea, open your mouths and spare not, and you shall be laden with sheaves upon your backs, for lo, I am with you (D&C 33:7–9).

"Sheaves" means convert baptisms. When you open your mouths, you'll be bringing these people to Christ.

> Yea, open your mouths and they shall be filled, saying: Repent, repent, and prepare ye the way of the Lord, and make his paths straight; for the kingdom of heaven is at hand; Yea, repent and be baptized, every one of you, for a remission of your sins; yea, be baptized even by water, and then cometh the baptism of fire and of the Holy Ghost" (D&C 33:10–11).

Our job is to overcome our fears so we can find people to bless. Many are "kept from the truth because they know not where to find it" (D&C 123:12). As missionaries and members, we are to find those who want to hear the word of the Lord. We made commitments at baptism that we would stand as witnesses of God at all times, and in all places, and in all things (see Mosiah 18:8–9). It is our duty. As full-time proselyting missionaries, we must understand that if we just have the courage, and overcome fear and doubt, then we can open our mouths, and they will be filled.

OVERCOMING FEAR

I'll never forget when I served as a mission president in the MTC. The last meeting before the missionaries would go out, I would speak about being bold, obedient, full of love, and courageous in opening their mouths. "Do not be afraid. The worth of souls is great. You have a mighty role in the kingdom." Well, some of them were still afraid. I would ask them on their way to their mission to have a finding experience of opening their mouth. This sweet young sister wrote me a letter after she'd been out two weeks, and this is how it went: "Dear President, after your talk Sunday night I was so nervous I didn't know what to do. I knew I'd be leaving Wednesday, and I was going to have to open my mouth. And I thought, *I can't do it, I can't do it.* So, I fasted and I prayed and I left Wednesday on the plane, and to my joy I had a window seat and my companion sat next to me. So I said, 'Oh dear I won't be able to talk to anybody on the plane,' and so I was relieved. But then, I got into the airport and I sat down, and here was a man sitting across from me. He was old and different looking, and I didn't know what to do. And all I could remember was your voice telling us, 'Open your mouths, it will be filled, I promise you.' Well, I girded up my loins and I opened my mouth and said, 'Hi, where you headed?' From that little beginning began an hour conversation. Pretty soon we became friends. And after a bit I said, 'If you knew there was another book written about Jesus Christ would you be interested in reading that? The Book of Mormon?'

He said, 'Oh, I have a Book of Mormon.' I committed him right there to read the book, and then he told me, 'My daughter is taking the discussions, too.'

And then I said, 'Is it OK if I have the missionaries come by and see you?' He said, 'That will just be fine.' Oh, President, it's so easy to open your mouth. The Lord will fill it. There's nothing to it." I read that letter every time to departing missionaries because it helped them realize that we can all do it. All of us, member missionary and full-time proselyting missionaries, can open our mouths and they will be filled.

Sometimes as missionaries we are afraid to do our duty. We just can't do it. Fear and doubt have overcome us. Missionaries who had the hardest time in the mission field were the ones who were afraid, who were filled with doubt, and who thought they couldn't do it. So we have to learn how to overcome fear. Fear and doubt can be overcome with five things: faith, love, knowledge, preparation, and experience.

Faith in the Lord Jesus Christ

If you exercise faith and mentally exert that power, fear and doubt will flea away. The apostles of old asked the Savior to increase their faith (see Luke 17:5). Faith comes by hearing the word of the Lord. Every time you read the scriptures, every time you hear your president speak, every time you talk together as companionships, or listen to your mom and dad, the word of the Lord will come into your heart and your faith will increase, and you'll become like Nephi and Lehi, the sons of Helaman, whose faith was so strong that they converted thousands of people (see Ether 12:14). Faith destroys doubt and fear. "They did fast and pray oft, and did wax stronger and stronger in their humility, and firmer and firmer in [their] faith" (Helaman 3:35). Faith is the first step toward decreasing your fear.

Love

Perfect love casteth out all fear (see 1 John 4:18). Think about it. If you're full of love, then there's no room for fear. When love is in your heart, how you feel about the worth of souls is overwhelming. You will have such concern that you will do anything to help them come unto Christ—you won't fear doing a single thing. Such was the example of the sons of Mosiah in their concern for their fellowmen (see Mosiah 28:3).

Knowledge

Knowledge is power. When you see and understand, you know what's out there and you're never afraid. I remember when I was little; I'd say, "Can you leave the light on just a little bit?" And then I wouldn't be quite so afraid. But then one time when I was a little boy we saw a bad movie. It was something like *Frankenstein Meets the Werewolf with the Mummy*. I know that sounds funny, I mean, now it would be a G-rated movie and we'd say, "Oh look how funny it is"; but in those days I was just a little nine-year-old boy, and I hid behind the seats. At that same time we lived on a farm. To irrigate our orchards we would receive water from Strawberry Reservoir. The time when it was our turn to receive the irrigation water was called a "water turn." Well, this one time it came at midnight. Now, my duty as the youngest boy, the baby of the family, was to do whatever my big brothers said. So my job was to go down to the end of the furrow, and when the water got there, say, "The water's here," and that's all I had to do. But, you must understand, it's midnight and there's a full moon. You know the werewolf is going to come; he's going to be there—there's no way out of it. So I started walking down the row, and the pheasants are flying by, and I thought, *Heavenly Father, I'm going to be a good boy. Don't let me die.* I was afraid. Why was I so afraid? Because I couldn't see. There was no light. I was afraid because of the past experience of that movie. When you get enough knowledge, when you see clearly, you will have power, and then fear will flee from you. That's how knowledge overpowers fear.

Preparation

"If ye are prepared ye shall not fear" (D&C 38:30). When you're prepared, fear is overcome. Preparation, like knowledge, is power. Self-confidence and self-reliance increase with our level of preparation.

When the vision and desire are in place, preparation becomes the master. It takes time, effort, dedication, and often sacrifice in order to prepare well. Make yourself fully capable of doing all that is required.

Be sure you are spiritually, emotionally, and mentally prepared with every needful thing. The greatest act of preparation is to form an uncompromising vision of being successful at the objectives you have committed yourself to achieve.

Make a detailed checklist of things you need to do in your preparation. Preparation means that you design and lay out a detailed plan for achieving what you desire. What are the target goals, objectives, deadlines, and milestones? Select target dates along the way to be sure your preparation is on schedule. How will you know you have succeeded? By measuring and evaluating as you go. Make mid-course corrections as you go—preparation is an ongoing process.

Preparation on the mission also has this vital dimension: you must have teamwork to be successful. Plan as a companionship.

Preparation is more important than we sometimes realize. We must make preparation in all things a permanent part of our lives. We must organize well so that preparation and planning get adequate time to help us achieve our goals. With this aspect of our mission in place, we will feel more in control, fear will not be part of our lives, and we can expect greater success. Make a goal to prepare well, and then enjoy the blessing of success in your life.

Experience

The more you do a thing the more your fear decreases. When new missionaries spent their first full day in our mission, the assistants to the president would teach them the dialogues and how to open their mouths. Then we'd send them out on the streets to meet people, just to open their mouths. The experience was something like this: "Would you be so kind and friendly as to answer a few questions that could bless your life? It'll only take a minute." That was the big number one question, after which we asked questions about life, our Savior, family, the Book of Mormon, etc. But, it was just that simple, "Hi, would you be so kind and friendly as to answer a few questions?" And after one day the experience helped conquer their fear. When we recognize that we are instruments in God's hands, disciples of Jesus Christ and filled with love, we can open our mouths.

BUILDING RELATIONSHIPS OF TRUST

When we are finding people to teach, we need to build relationships of trust. Sometimes we need to remember that when we begin the personal contacting phase of opening our mouths, we must remember who we are and what we radiate. We have an aura about us. The body is only the house in which we live. God helps us to radiate strength, control, love, charity, consideration, and best wishes for all human beings. We should do what we can to produce peace and harmony. We radiate this love as missionaries.

How's our general appearance? Are our white shirts cleaned and pressed? Do we look good in our blouses and skirts sisters? Do we look pleasing? Do we have a smile? What do we radiate? In our conversations, do we build on similar interests, common concerns and beliefs, and especially gospel topics? Do we ask appropriate questions void of offense? Here is an example of how to start building on common grounds: "Is a close, strong family important to you?"

They say, "Well oh yes, I love my kids. One is in Cub Scouts, another one is in scouting, and they're so good."

"Oh really, we have scouting in our church too, that's so great. Would you mind if we came over and told you about our family home evening program?" And then all of a sudden you're there. What I just said has happened thousands of times. You must ask the appropriate question, and you must open your mouth and start a gospel conversation so someone will want to hear about the gospel of Jesus Christ. If we fail to open our mouths, we fail to share the gospel.

When you win their hearts you will be like Ammon. I always wanted to be like Ammon. When Ammon goes to King Lamoni he's in the finding mode; he's opening his mouth. He greets King Lamoni, "Thanks for untying me; I'm grateful you took me out of jail. Could I just be your servant for a while?"

King Lamoni answers, "Well, you look so nice; here—have one of my daughters to wife."

"No thanks, I just want to be your servant."

"Wonderful, would you go out and guard my sheep? I need someone to guard my sheep."

And as you know the story, in come the wicked, wicked Lamanites to scare away the king's flock. Well, the Lamanite guards are scared, they say, "Oh no, the king will be upset."

And Ammon says, "This is so good. Now I can show forth the power of God that I might win their hearts so they'll listen to what I have to say" (see Alma 17:29). There is a process where you must build trust, love, and respect to a point that they're willing to listen to you. Sometimes it might take a thirty-minute conversation to find someone who will be willing to let you teach them. Sometimes it might just be a call-back appointment. But the important thing is that we open our mouths at all times, and in all places, and in all things.

Alma 26:29 indicates that we should open our mouths on the streets and in the synagogues; and Doctrine and Covenants 24:12 tells us to open our mouths everywhere we go and at all times. You don't go anywhere without opening your mouth. Everywhere, at all times, in all things, in all places—on the streets, at the bus stop, as you're walking down the street, as you're standing at the bus stop, in the bus, and as you're going through the line at the grocery store. There are hundreds of people every day that you pass by, and you have to open your mouth, and all will be blessed because you do.

THE POWER OF WORKING TOGETHER

Read John 15:16, and pay particular attention to the phrase, that "your fruit should remain." It isn't enough to teach with power and baptize. You have to make sure that your fruit remains. Why are you learning the six new-member discussions? Because those discussions are imperative for the retention of new members. There are other ways to help your converts stay converted. Make sure you go with a member or ask a stake missionary to come with you to give those lessons. This is vital! If you don't take a member with you, the convert will probably have a hard time making the social connection with the members.

Besides helping new converts, don't overlook the power of working with members to find new investigators. If you want extra power, delegation is a great tool for getting things accomplished. God the Father delegated the creation of the earth to His son, Jehovah, who, with Michael and others, organized this earth from material that had always existed. Then, under the direction of the Father, our first parents were created.

I believe in delegation; I believe that many hands make light work. If I were on a mission, I would work with members in the ward or branch where I was serving. I'd find five or ten people, and I'd develop relationships of trust with them. I'd visit them, get to know them, prove my righteousness, and let them see my sincere desire.

Then I'd approach them. Every member is a result of missionary work, and most members have had a missionary experience. Share your own missionary experiences with members. Ask them to share their conversion story with you. Tell them about one of the people you've just recently converted. Tell them about the greatest work in the world. Tell them what a joy it is to work with people who are eager to hear about the gospel. Tell them how wonderful it is to be associated with people who are searching for the truth. As we share these missionary experiences, the Spirit of the Lord will come upon us.

When investigators are taught in members' homes you will be highly successful. So be sure and schedule enough time in your mission to visit members, to inspire them, to love them, to motivate them, to commit them to setting a date to prepare a friend. And you can only do that when they trust you and love you and respect you. You must have the same attitude of patience and love with the members that you do with your investigators.

Once, when I was a mission president, I met with the elders quorum president, and I said, "Hi there, how are you doing? Will you do this? Will you do that? I'm the mission president; will you give me these names?"

And he said, "Who is this wild man?" And he didn't like me.

And I thought, *Why don't you want to be a missionary? Everyone's supposed to be a missionary.* I became sad and upset. It was my third week as the mission president in England, and I was praying. I said, "Heavenly Father," and I began to cry. "This isn't fair. They're not doing their part. I'm working and no one wants to work, and this isn't right."

And then a voice came to me, and the voice said, "Ed my son, I didn't ask you to come here to judge them; I asked you to come here to love them." My heart was softened and my life changed in a moment. Love the members. Love them so much that they will feel the Spirit that you feel. You love them so much that they'll want to love like you do; they'll feel like the sons of Mosiah. They won't be able to bear that any human soul should endure endless torment. You will know when charity is in your heart, as missionaries and members, because you'll want to share the gospel with your fellowmen.

In that desire to share the gospel, when your investigators are coming along well, invite them to invite their friends—they are fearless. They'll invite everybody. Especially invite your new converts to share the gospel with their fellowmen. You want them to be enthused about the gospel so they'll keep living it day after day. We also want to help members become enthused. We want them to help in every way. Read Alma 6:6 and 3 Nephi 18:19–23 with these members, then invite them to help you with your work. Ask them to help you find people to teach, to help you friendship and fellowship the people you are teaching now.

During a mission presidents' seminar in June of 1980, President Kimball promised Church members that if they would pray night and morning regarding their desire to see other people join the Church, the Lord would hear their prayers and soften the hearts of the people they associate with. Invite your member friends to pray every day for this blessing, and promise them that when they pray with all their hearts, with real intent, they'll see a difference as the hearts of their friends and associates are touched and softened.

OBEDIENCE

It's kind of interesting how, when we understand the vision of the work, life changes. My dear friend Cyril Figuerres said these words:

"Obedience is the price, faith is the power, love is the motive, the Spirit is the key, for Christ is the reason." When we know what Christ has done for us, we will want to open our mouths, and they will be filled with everything we need to say. The Lord will indeed bless us. The law of the harvest is there:

> There is a law, irrevocably decreed in heaven before the foundations of this world, upon which all blessings are predicated—and when we obtain any blessing from God, it is by obedience to that law upon which it is predicated (D&C 130:20–21).

This law is to open your mouth, and it will be filled, and blessings will be yours.

The Lord cautioned us:

> But with some I am not well pleased, for they will not open their mouths, but they hide the talent which I have given unto them, because of the fear of man. Wo unto such, for mine anger is kindled against them. And it shall come to pass, if they are not more faithful unto me, it shall be taken away, even that which they have (D&C 60:2–3).

We must overcome our fears so that we can preach with power and find Heavenly Father's children. They too can then enjoy the gospel of Jesus Christ.

When we open our mouths, sometimes we don't know exactly what to say. So in our mission there was a rule, you could not pass anyone on the street without saying, "Excuse me, would you be so kind and friendly as to answer a few questions?" And pretty soon, all the missionaries understood, and all of a sudden baptisms weren't thirty a month, but they were 130 a month. Why? Because the Lord blessed the missionaries because they were obedient.

Here is one of the most beautiful parts of the process. If you've studied, if you've pleaded with the Lord, and if you're worthy and desire righteousness—you're being obedient—then words and ideas will come out of your mouth that you've never even known.

The other day I was speaking to a group, and afterwards a man came up to me and said, "That was the most profound statement I've ever heard in my life."

"What was?" I asked.

"When you said that truth without testimony is hollow." He had it written down on a piece of paper.

"Wow," I said. "Who said that?"

"You did."

"When?" I asked.

"Just now, in that room."

"Can I write that down?" So I wrote it down, and now I'm sharing it with you. And why was I able to say that? Because the Lord inspires us; sometimes we don't even realize what we've said! President Marion G. Romney once observed that he always knew when he had spoken by the Spirit because he learned from what he had said (qtd. by Boyd K. Packer, *Teach Ye Diligently*, 356).

When we exercise our faith, the Lord will bless us. If our faith is sufficient, those beyond the veil, under the direction of Jesus Christ, will assist us in our missionary labors (see D&C 49:27 and Mor. 7:30–31). I believe that; I know it's true.

Even when we don't know exactly what to say, if the words we utter reflect the feelings of our hearts, the strength of our character, and the depth of our testimony, then the Lord will help us. President Monson promised us that "whom the Lord calls, the Lord qualifies" (*Live the Good Life*, 121).

THE LORD'S PROMISE

I will never forget two sisters. It was a dark, dark night in the heart of London. So dark that they were nervous. A man came up by them at the bus stop, a large man, a dark man, and they were nervous. And then they said they remembered what President Pinegar said, "Don't fear, the Lord is before your face. He's on your right hand, he's on your left hand, His Spirit is in your heart, His angels round about you" (see D&C 84:88). So these two sister missionaries spoke. "Excuse me sir, would you be so kind and friendly as to answer a few questions that might bring you happiness."

And he said, "Well, I'd be glad to young ladies." And he did. He was from the Solomon Islands. He was in England for four weeks. He heard the message, and, since the sisters cannot teach a man alone, they went to the church. And later this man, Peter Salaka, said, "I want to meet your President." So I went with them on a discussion. Peter Salaka is an elect man of God; just like we learn in the Doctrine and Covenants, that the elect shall hear his voice and know that it's true (see D&C 29:7). These two sisters taught him. We arranged for a baptism. Peter Salaka spoke at his own baptism. It was the greatest talk I have ever heard at a baptism. It was like he was a bishop already, like he'd been in the Church all of his life. I thought, *Who is this man?* They took him to church on Sunday, interviewed him, and ordained him to the office of a priest after having conferred the Aaronic Priesthood upon him. He then left for the Solomon Islands, which was in one of the Australian missions at the time. I called the Australian mission president and informed him of the baptism of Peter Salaka, who lived in the Solomon Islands. He said, "That's great, that's part of our mission, I think we have one member there on that island. We'll see what we can do."

I said, "Just make sure you make contact with him, I've given him your name, your phone number, and your address. Here's his address back in the Solomon Islands; please write him and follow up. I'll do the same." Time went by, and Elder Sonnenberg, of the Quorum of the Seventy, who was the President of the Australian area, and Elder Faust, then a member of the Twelve, went on a visit to the Solomon Islands to see what they could do to start the branches there. Peter Salaka greeted them at the airport. "I am Peter Salaka, and this is my son. I am a priest in The Church of Jesus Christ of Latter-day Saints. How can I help you build up the Church here?" Elder Sonnenberg sent me a picture of Elder Faust, himself, and Brother Salaka. Where would he be if those two magnificent sisters had not opened their mouths? If we allow one person to walk by and not open our mouth, we deprive them of the opportunity of exaltation. This isn't a business; this is a matter of spiritual life and death. I am grateful that those faithful sisters opened their mouths, so that they could be the instruments in the hands of the Lord to bless that great brother.

We must do personal contacting on a daily basis. There is time to personally contact every day. Make it your goal to open your mouth with every single person you see or come in contact with. "Excuse me, would you be so kind . . .?" Make sure you open your mouth. Do not be afraid. You'll never know who will be a golden contact. You would never want to judge who that might be. But if you're dedicated, the Lord will help you find them.

Now, for missionaries to get members to do this, we need a relationship of trust with those members. We need to present them a message about the worth of souls, and how important members are in the conversion process—how important it is to friendship and fellowship investigators and new converts. You've got to make sure that the members are converted to doing this. Elder Ballard taught us to "set a date" to find someone to teach; and when he did, I thought, *Well, I'm a member too. I've got to find somebody.* So I set a date. And I remember a name came into my mind—Jeff Lewis, he was the one. So I came back from that fireside that week, and I said to my missionary preparation class, "You know, I know just the person, and I've got the date, but I don't know where he is. He was here at UVSC, but he's gone. I haven't seen him for a year." I said, "Jeff Lewis is his name. Do any of you know someone by that name?"

What was the mathematical probability of that happening? A boy in the class raised his hand and he said, "Oh, Jeff Lewis? I know him. He's a nonmember. He lives with my best friend down at BYU."

I said, "Are you serious?"

He said, "Yes."

I said, "Can you give me his phone number?"

He said, "Of course."

That week I got Jeff Lewis's phone number and called him. "Jeff, this is Brother Ed."

"Brother Ed, my friend." We were friends because I taught him as a nonmember at the institute and he had the discussions, but then he moved. So I had to find him again.

I said, "Jeff, I want to talk to you. Would you be so kind and friendly as to come and see me?" Jeff came out to my office. We visited three times. I challenged him and he was baptized. On January 12, 1997, I baptized Jeff Lewis at BYU and spoke at his baptism. What if Elder Ballard hadn't spoken? What if I hadn't opened my mouth in class and said, "Who knows Jeff Lewis?" And lo and behold, what did the Lord do? He arranged for somebody to be in class that day; someone who knew where Jeff lived and knew his roommate. And oh, by the way, to make it a little easier for me, He made sure he had his phone number so I could call him.

CONCLUSION

Do you believe now? Do you believe that whenever you open your mouth it will be filled? It is so easy. Plead with the Lord to soften the hearts of the people so they will receive you. Exercise your faith. The Lord promised that He would go before you to prepare the hearts and minds of the people to accept the gospel. He will lead you to those that are prepared.

⟜ 𝒞HAPTER 9 ⟞

MISSIONARY DIALOGUES

So, now that we've opened our mouths, what kind of questions do we ask, how do we start a gospel conversation, how do we build that relationship of trust? The following examples are dialogues that will give you ideas about how to start, and finish, gospel conversations, make appointments, build positive relationships with your investigators, place copies of the Book of Mormon, resolve your investigators' concerns, and help them commit to baptism.

STARTING A GOSPEL CONVERSATION

Remember to start with positive labeling so your contact feels more inclined to listen to what you have to say. Start on the street: "Would you be so kind and friendly as to answer a few questions that could bring you happiness?" Or how about at a bus stop or in a grocery line: "Hello—you look like someone with a minute to spare—we're asking people just a few questions about life, and you can usually answer yes or no, alright? Great! The first question is . . . " Here's a door approach: "Hello, nice to see you! My name's ___ and this is my companion ___, and what we're doing today is talking with a few people, asking some questions that could bring you happiness. Could you spare a minute? Wonderful!"

The important idea is to be friendly and warm, and give them the feeling that you only need to talk with them for just a moment, just to help you answer a few questions that could bless their lives. The following chart presents questions that can start gospel conversations on various topics: the purpose of life, families, the mission of Jesus Christ, prophets, and the scriptures.

Questions That Can Start a Gospel Conversation

Purpose of Life

1. Do you believe there's a plan for earth life?
2. Do you feel all people are a part of that plan?
3. Do you feel as though you're a part of that plan?
4. What is the purpose of life?
5. What would make you happier?

Families

1. Is a close, strong family important to you?
2. Do you believe the world is tearing families apart?
3. Do you believe families that pray together stay together?
4. What could make your family more united?

Mission of Jesus Christ

1. Do you believe in the prophets of the Old Testament?
2. Why did Christ come to earth?
3. What has Christ done for you?
4. Do you follow Christ's teachings?
5. Would you like to follow his teachings better?

Prophets

1. Do you believe in the prophets of the Old Testament?
2. Do you believe that God cares about you as much as the people in Old Testament times?
3. If there was a prophet today, would you follow him?
4. How would you know if he was a true prophet?

Scriptures

1. Do you believe in the scriptures?
2. Do you read them? (How often?)
3. How can we know that the scriptures are true?
4. If you knew there was another book of scripture concerning Jesus Christ, would you read it?

AVOIDING CALL-BACK DISAPPOINTMENTS

You will save a lot of time, hassle, and disappointment if you remember these suggestions on how to get return appointments:

- Ask for a telephone number.
- Ask directions (bus routes, nearest train stations, familiar landmarks, etc.).
- Tell them it's a long way for you to travel, but if you leave at a certain time you should just make it (that way they are more likely to be there).
- Ask them to spell the street and repeat the address.
- Express the importance of the message, your excitement to see them, and that you plan to be there only thirty minutes.
- Wait for them to correct you or say OK.
- Give them a pamphlet or card with the appointment time, and your names and telephone number on it.
- Ask them to call if something unexpected comes up.
- DON'T FORGET TO ASK THE REFERRAL INVITATION!!!
- If possible, call to confirm the appointment before you go.
- Always pray for inspiration to do and say what the Lord would have you do.

When you go to visit a call back, you'll want to approach with the knowledge that the person you're coming to see has already expressed interest in learning more. There's no need to ask them if they are still interested. Rather, be positive and enthusiastic and say something like: "Hello Mr. Leavitt! It's good to see you again. I'm ___ and this is ___. You helped us out last Saturday in town by answering a few questions about your family and some of your basic beliefs. Because of your answers, we would like to share a short message with you."

If the people don't seem quite as interested as they were when you questioned them on the street, just show extra enthusiasm and get them to remember their earlier interest. Try something like this:

"Remember how interesting this question was, and the idea you had about why we're here on earth? Well, this little message we have today only takes a few minutes and will answer that question you have, as well as many others. May we please come in and share that with you?"

Also, the person to whom you asked the questions may not be home, but try something like this with whoever is at home: "Hello, ma'am! We visited with John the day before yesterday, and he was very interested in what we asked him. We would sure like to visit with you as well. Could we come in?"

At times you may be at the incorrect address. If that occurs, *always* ask a few questions of the person who lives at the address. For example, "I'm sorry, we must have gotten an incorrect address. But say—we're sure glad you're home so we didn't make an unnecessary journey. Would you be so kind as to answer a few questions?"

HOW TO KEEP GOING IN THE RIGHT DIRECTION

Remember, our goal is to find children of God to teach the gospel to, by obtaining call backs or teaching discussions; and then bring them to the waters of baptism when they are converted. The best way to start getting there is to build that relationship of trust—to really understand our investigators, to find out their strong feelings on important gospel issues, and to be able to answer their questions. If we do this, then we can direct our first discussion in a way that helps our investigators to get the most out of it.

The following concepts will help you find ways to build a trusting relationship, as well as effectively move the conversation forward. Look for examples of how they are used in the sample dialogues following this list. (1) Always build on common beliefs. (2) Genuinely compliment them when they give a positive answer. (3) Tell them how you have had a similar feeling, and share personal experiences that validate that claim. (4) When they tell you how they feel, use the IF—THEN formula: if they care about God, then surely they want to hear about Him; if they care about families, then surely they'll want to hear about how to strengthen their family; if they would want to read a book written by prophets who testify of Christ, then surely they will want to read the Book of Mormon, etc.

When you study the following sample dialogues, remember to adapt everything to your own personality and mannerisms and the needs of your investigators. And most importantly, follow the Spirit.

Families

Families are a good place to start a gospel conversation. "Is a close family important to you?" If they say yes, then continue on with the discussion. "I'm so glad a strong family is important to you. How many children do you have? Oh, that is great! We have ___ children in my family. Do you feel you could be with your family forever? Would you like to be? That's great! In fact, we want to share a little message that talks about the importance of families, especially today in this world where families are struggling to stay close. There are some things you can do to strengthen your family even more . . . ." Here's another approach to the question. "Should churches provide better programs for families and the youth? Do you belong to any church now? That's good, you know, I feel like you do. The churches really should have programs to help families. The church I belong to, The Church of Jesus Christ of Latter-day Saints, has a program called 'family home evening' that families hold each Monday night in our homes. Through that program, families can learn how to draw closer together and learn to love more, learn to be more obedient to our Father in Heaven, and learn how to become happier . . . ."

Prophets

"Do you believe God cares about you as much as He cared about people in Old Testament times?" Most people would respond positively to this question. So if they do, then continue with something like this: "I believe like you do. Do you think He would want His children today to hear His words and understand what to do in these days to be happy? Of course He would. We have the most exciting message in the world to share today, to help people understand how our Heavenly Father deals with man today, just as He did before. And did you know that right here in this day and age, God has spoken to man and restored His priesthood . . . ."

Scriptures

"Do you believe the Bible to be the word of God, or just a history?" If your investigators answer that they believe it to be the word of God, then continue with a more pointed question: "I believe the same. Well, tell me, if you knew there was another book of scripture, written by the prophets, that also testifies of Christ—would you read it?" They've already admitted that the scriptures are important, so they would be hard pressed to answer "no" to a question like that. That's when you continue with your message. "You would?! That's wonderful. The message we've been sharing today includes such a book. It's called the Book of Mormon. It is another testament of Jesus Christ. It tells how Heavenly Father deals with His children on earth, including those who lived in the ancient Americas, who were given the gospel—by Christ—after His resurrection . . . ."

The Mission of Jesus Christ

"Do you believe in Jesus Christ?" If they are already Christian, then this question is a good place to build on common beliefs. "Excellent. You know, many people today don't believe Jesus Christ is the Son of God. The fact that you do means you probably have a personal relationship with Jesus already, and that you probably want to live your life according to His commandments. We have a short presentation that tells you about the plan our Heavenly Father has for us with His son Jesus Christ . . . ."

The Purpose of Life

Asking about the purpose of life is probably the easiest way to start a dialogue and find out where your investigators are coming from. Most people, no matter what their religion or background, have probably wondered about why they are here, or how they can be happier, how to cope with death or crisis, or whether God exists. Start with any of these topics, and go from there: "If there were any question you could ask God, what would that be?" Or "Would you like to be happier?" If they say they would like to be happier, or mention concerns about the purpose of life (why they're here, where they came from, where they are going after this life), then continue with the dialogue and answer their questions.

"You know, some of those questions trouble all of us." Maybe you could share a personal experience here, or how a loved one found an answer to a difficult question. "I've discovered that there are answers to those questions. Our Heavenly Father does have a plan to help us discover what our purpose is, and how we can be happier. We would love to share a short message about that plan with you . . . ."

Here's one with prayer as the subject. "Is prayer an effective way for you to communicate with God?" If they say "yes," then build on that common belief. "You know, there are many people on the earth today who feel like you and I do about prayer." If they say "no," then explain why you feel it is an effective way to communicate. "Well, you know, I've had my prayers answered . . . ." Another question could be, "Have you ever thought about praying over which church is true? You have? Well, we have a short presentation about how one young man's prayer was answered on which church to join . . . ."

Or how about this approach: "Have you thought about praying for help and guidance to do what Heavenly Father would want you to do? We have a short presentation that talks about God's plan for us and how we can communicate with Him to know what we should do with our lives. We would love to show you how prayer makes a difference, and we have a story about a young man who wanted to know . . . ."

The problem of pain and sorrow is one of the hardest things for people to understand. How could a loving God allow people to suffer? If the Spirit directs you, or if your investigator brings up the subject, then you might want to approach the issue with a question like this—if they haven't already asked it of you: "How do you cope with death or a major crisis in your life?" The answer would be most effective if coupled with sensitivity to what might be going on in your investigators' lives, and a personal story; if appropriate, a personal experience lets them know that you understand their crisis. "It's hard, isn't it? I guess there is only one way we can cope with that, and that's with the strength of the Lord, and knowing that God has a purpose for us. When I was younger . . . and that's how I came to be here with you. I'd like to share what I've learned because it means so much to me, and brings me so much peace. We have a short little presentation to help people understand death and resurrection, and the life here-after . . . ."

RESOLVING CONCERNS

There are times when an investigator expresses concerns, doubts, and objections. What should you do if they do not agree with what you have been saying? Or if they become angry with you? Resolving concerns becomes necessary at many different times.

Be sincerely interested in people even if they disagree with you. Do not become defensive, or insensitive to their needs and feelings. Always keep and build on the positive. Make sure you are trying to help them resolve their concerns and accept the truth. You should recognize that investigators' expressions of concern, confusion, or fear are very valuable to you in your teaching. If your investigators have these feelings, it gives you a good opportunity to *understand* them, and to be *understood* in your teachings.

You should resolve concerns by listening with empathy, and then prepare them for continued teaching. To do this, you should find out their level of understanding and acceptance of the principle taught. Ask questions like: "How do you feel about what we have discussed?" Or, "Do you see why we live the Word of Wisdom?" You also need to learn *why* they have that concern or doubt so you can help them resolve it. Ask them for reasons: "What makes you uncomfortable?"

In resolving their doubts, explain why you believe in the principles discussed. For example, "We believe that the Book of Mormon is true because the Holy Ghost bears witness of its truthfulness." Use scriptures, personal experiences, and testimonies to improve their understanding.

Maybe you could write the concerns down on a blank piece of paper. Then, as you discuss and resolve them, cross them out so everyone understands that the concern no longer exists.

THE SOFT CHALLENGE AND SIX-DISCUSSION COMMITMENT

Soft Challenge: "If you knew these things were true, would you follow Jesus Christ and be baptized?" This is one of the greatest questions you can ask—and you can ask it several times. You will normally ask it at the end of the first discussion. You might say something like this: "Mr. Jones, thank you so much for letting us share this message with you today. We know these things are true, and want others to know as well. Let me ask you a question: "*If* you knew for yourself that the things we talked about today were true, would you follow Jesus Christ and be baptized?"

The best part about that question is that it follows the IF—THEN model. *If* a person knew it were true, *then* he or she *would* be baptized. You can then explain that it's your job as missionaries to help people come to this knowledge of the truth. It now becomes a *challenge* to the investigators to find out whether or not the message is true, and when they know for themselves, they have already said they are willing to be baptized.

So here's how to set up the next five appointments. "We usually share six presentations—you've heard the first one already. When you've heard all of our message you'll have a better understanding of the purpose of life and what you can do to be really happy. Are you normally home at this hour?" Now you've done two things: committed them to be baptized if they knew it was true, and set up appointments to hear the remaining five discussions.

THE "STRAIT GATE" DIALOGUE

After the second discussion, to keep our investigators thinking about commitments and working for baptism, utilize the "strait gate" dialogue. Explain the importance of goals—any example will do—and how they help us progress as we strive to reach them. Then explain that our main goal is to return to live with our Father in Heaven. Have them read that wonderful scripture in Matthew that talks about how to do that. "Enter ye in at the strait gate: for wide is the gate, and broad is the way, that leadeth to destruction, and many there be which go in thereat: Because strait is the gate, and narrow is the way, which leadeth unto life, and few there be that find it" (Matt. 7:13–14).

Then, launch into a discussion about the scripture: "How many paths are there? Where does the broad path go? How many will be on it? Where does the narrow one go? How many will be on it? Which one do you want to be on?"

At this point, you can ask what the gate is that gets us on the path back to God, and then read the answer in 2 Nephi 31:17 or John 3:5, the ones that talk about repentance, baptism, and receiving of the Holy Ghost as being that strait gate. Then set a date (a goal) to work for. Tell them that all they need to do is hear the discussions, attend church, read their scriptures and pray about the truthfulness of the message.

THE THIRD-DISCUSSION–COMMITMENT DIALOGUE

Let's suppose you have investigators who are not yet committed for baptism, even though you've given more than three discussions, soft challenged them, talked frequently about baptism, reviewed past commitments like reading and praying, and attempted the "strait gate" dialogue. You may find they're still unable to commit to a solid date because of a "hidden" concern. The following dialogues are like a heart-to-heart talk with your investigator, and should reveal and help resolve any remaining concerns, as well as help them to commit to a firm date.

Ask any, or all, of the following questions: (1) "How do you feel when we teach you? (2)What would be the hardest teaching to live?

(3) What good things would happen if you joined the Church? (4) Is there anything in the Church or its teachings that is evil and would cause a person to be bad? (5) Is there any reason why you shouldn't join the Church? (6) Is there anything that concerns you about relations, or anything general concerning membership in the Church?" If you get to the bottom of a concern, try to resolve it. And last, but not least, bear your testimony. "We know the Church is true and we want you to be happy with this knowledge."

Make sure they continue reading, attending church, and praying, and try to get them to receive a member visit. And, as directed by the Spirit, try to get a more solid commitment with questions like these: "Do you have a desire to repent and come to Christ? Will you promise to keep the commandments the best you can? Do you have a beginning testimony of the truthfulness of the Church and its teachings, and that Jesus is the Christ?" If they have such feelings and knowledge, then ask them again if they will be baptized.

OPPOSITION FROM FRIENDS AND RELATIVES

Most opposition is caused by misunderstanding. The best way to ease misunderstanding is to build relationships of trust. The questions need not be in order, but be sure to come to an agreement whenever possible. Begin with both parties telling each other how much you love and care about the investigator. Ask those giving opposition to your investigator some loving, caring, and tender questions—questions inspired by the Spirit.

Allow them to respond to your questions; don't correct them, but empathize with them. Respond by saying, "I see how you feel, we feel such and such a way, and Suzy feels the same way about it." Remember—if you are prepared, the Lord will bring to your memory the *what*, *why*, and *how* to say it by the power of the Holy Ghost. The following may give you ideas about how to approach the problem: (1) "How do you feel about Suzy? (2) What is the hardest teaching for you to accept? (3) What evil would come of Suzy living the teachings of the gospel? (4)What good things might come of Suzy's joining the Church? (5) Don't you think it's great that Suzy wants to live a clean and wholesome life, and that she feels so strongly about the Savior? (6) Just because Suzy wants to be baptized doesn't mean she doesn't love and care about you. She still wants to be your obedient child. (7) Suzy wants to be baptized on such and such a date; would you consider giving permission (or being supportive, if a friend or relative)?"

If the opposition is coming from friends rather than parents, ask them why they are discouraging their friend, and if they would please respect, with love, their friend's choice to be baptized. Remember, these discussions require the most sensitivity to the Spirit so that we don't make matters worse.

CALLING FOR BACKUP

When you've tried everything you can to calm your investigators', or their loved ones', concerns, then try calling for backup. Even after baptism, after you leave, new converts will need that community support. Outside pressure is one of the greatest causes of people not keeping their commitments and coming into the Church. The pointing, jeering finger of the spacious building claims many of Heavenly Father's children.

Have the bishop or another member visit with your investigators to help them resolve their concerns. Invite them to a ward activity, a social, or a Relief Society, Young Men's, Young Women's, or primary activity, or on a ward picnic—show them that there are people who love them that can support them. Remember that their concerns raise the level of doubt in their minds. This destroys faith. Therefore, you must consider it imperative to resolve such doubts. Only those whose faith is strong and firm in Jesus Christ can withstand such pressure. And bringing them into the fold of Jesus Christ is a good way to help nurture their growing testimonies.

CONCLUSION

As you work with each child of God, remember that everyone is an individual—we are all different. You need the Spirit to help you say the appropriate things. It is the Spirit that will help you say, and help them understand and believe, the words of God.

CHAPTER 10

USING THE BOOK OF MORMON AS THE
KEY TO CONVERSION

Although the prophets in Book of Mormon times wrote in the characters of reformed Egyptian, this is a book for our dispensation. Joseph Smith called the Book of Mormon the keystone to our religion, and then declared that "a man would get nearer to God by abiding by its precepts, than by any other book" ("Introduction," Book of Mormon).

If you know anything about building arches, you know that the keystone is the center piece of stone that holds the arch up. The purpose of the Book of Mormon is to witness that Heavenly Father is our Father and that He extends mercy and loves us; to witness of Jesus Christ; and to document how He has dealt with all of His people. This book is for you and me; it is written for members and nonmembers alike. If you learn to love it, this book will be the greatest power you have on your mission. If you learn to love and understand its teachings, you will then be able to testify of the book, and you will have great converting power.

A DIVINE WITNESS

The Book of Mormon was translated by the power of God through the Prophet Joseph Smith—who gave his life for this book. He was tarred and feathered and left for dead in Hyrum, Ohio; he was thrown in jail, and mocked and ridiculed just for bringing the book into existence. And Joseph wasn't the only prophet who suffered for the sake of the book. Abinadi was burned at the stake, and Moroni was left alone to preserve it when all his people had died. Because of the importance of the book, Enos prayed to the Lord with all of his heart that the book would come forth in this day. "Thy fathers have also required of me this thing," the Lord told Enos. "And it shall be done unto them according to their faith; for their faith was like unto thine" (Enos 1:18).

Why is the book so important? What is its purpose? The purpose of the Book of Mormon is fivefold: (1) it stands as a second testament or witness for Jesus Christ; (2) it authenticates the Bible; (3) it shows the goodness of God to His children; (4) it makes people aware of the promises that God has made to His children; (5) and it restores to earth many plain and precious truths that were lost during the apostasy.

The first purpose, however, is primary. This book convinces people, both members and nonmembers, that Jesus is the Christ. "Come unto Christ, and be perfected in him" (Moroni 10:32) the scriptures invite. That is the purpose of the Book of Mormon. That is what you must know, that is what you must feel, that is what you must understand. That knowledge of the book must be radiating from your very being. This is one of the reasons that you are instructed to sup from these pages for thirty minutes every day. You will never be the missionary you were destined to be until you love and live this book. It is the key to your converting power. It is the key to your retaining power.

LOVING AND LIVING BY THE BOOK

The Book of Mormon will never become part of your life until you delight in the word of God. "Now, we will compare the word [the Book of Mormon is the word of God] unto a seed," Alma teaches; "Now, if ye give place, that a seed may be planted in your heart" (Alma 32:28), or in other words, we take this seed, this word of God, this Book of Mormon, and put it in our hearts. (It might help to know that in Hebrew the word *heart* is *leb* or *lebab*, which interpreted means the center of the mind or the center of the soul, the decision-making center of your body; so when we yield our hearts to the Lord, what we're doing is saying, "All my decisions are the decisions Thou would make, Father. Not my will, but Thy will.")

Now back to Alma. If we give a place for the seed, which is the Book of Mormon, to be planted in our hearts (or in other words, all of our decisions will be made by the principles contained in the book), then:

> If it be a true seed, or a good seed, if ye do not cast it out by your unbelief, that ye will resist the Spirit of the Lord, behold, it will begin to swell within your breasts; and when you feel these swelling motions, ye will begin to say within yourselves—It must needs be that this is a good seed, or that the word is good, for it beginneth to enlarge my soul; yea, it beginneth to enlighten my understanding, yea, it beginneth to be delicious to me (Alma 32:28).

When the Book of Mormon lives in our lives, then we will be pure disciples of Christ with great converting power, fulfilling the destiny that President Ezra Taft Benson described so eloquently when he said:

> I have a vision of homes alerted, of classes alive, of pulpits aflame with the Spirit of the Book of Mormon message . . . I have a vision of the whole Church getting nearer to God by abiding the precepts of the Book of Mormon" ("Flooding the Earth with the Book of Mormon," *Ensign*, Nov. 1988, 4–6).

President Benson has also said, "The Book of Mormon . . . needs to become more central in our preaching, our teaching, and our missionary work" ("Flooding the Earth with the Book of Mormon," *Ensign*, Nov. 1988, 4–6). He counseled us to flood the earth with the Book of Mormon, adding this call to action:

> I challenge our mission leaders to show their missionaries how to challenge their contacts to read the Book of Mormon and

pray about it . . . I challenge the homes of Israel to display on
their walls great quotations and scenes from the Book of
Mormon ("Flooding the Earth with the Book of Mormon,"
Ensign, Nov. 1988, 4–6).

In early Church history, some missionaries returned from their
missions and were reproved. "You have treated lightly the things you
have received," they were told. "Which vanity and unbelief have
brought the whole Church under condemnation" (D&C 84:54–55).
Said Elder Bruce R. McConkie:

> The Book of Mormon contains that portion of the Lord's
> word which is needed to prove the divinity of His great latter-day
> work, and which is needed to teach the basic doctrines of salva-
> tion to mankind" ("This Generation Shall Have My Word,"
> *Ensign*, June 1980, 54).

And during General Conference in 1960, President Marion G. Romney
said, "The Book of Mormon is the most effective piece of missionary litera-
ture we have" (*Conference Report*, April 1960, 110). In using this powerful
book with our investigators, we have the promise of President Ezra Taft
Benson: "The Lord will manifest the truthfulness of it, by the power of the
Holy Ghost" ("The Message: Of the Most Worth," *New Era*, June 1989).

A POWERFUL TOOL OF CONVERSION

It's important that you and I develop an abiding faith in the Lord's
promise that if people will ask with a sincere heart, having faith in
Christ, the truthfulness of the Book of Mormon will be given to them
(see Moroni 10:3–5). Think about what it means to our investigators if
they can accept the Book of Mormon in their lives: if the Book of
Mormon is true, then Joseph Smith was a prophet; if Joseph Smith was
a prophet, the First Vision really did take place; if the First Vision was a
reality, the priesthood was restored; if the priesthood was restored, the
Doctrine and Covenants, Pearl of Great Price, and other scriptures are
true; not only that, but the Church, which was established by Joseph

Smith, is true; and so we're led by true prophets of the Lord today. They will know all that when they accept the Book of Mormon!

This is what we must ingrain in our very souls: the Book of Mormon is the tool that will retain converts better than any other thing. If we root the people to our sociality, or friendliness, or love, we root them to us instead of to Christ. That happens sometimes because missionaries are so loving and so good.

But that's exactly why we must put the Book of Mormon first. If we root them to that holy book of scripture, our converts will be retained long after we leave. I'm sure you've heard of converts who left the Church as soon as "their" missionaries were transferred. That doesn't happen when converts have come unto Christ, because coming unto Christ goes much deeper than simple friendship. You see, loving Christ is the essence of conversion. We are converted to Jesus Christ by the power of the Holy Ghost, which is felt as we study and pray about the Book of Mormon, because the Book of Mormon is a sure witness and testament that Jesus is the Christ. Any other root will wither.

When we root our converts in the love of the people, or the love of the Church, or the love of the sociality and friendships they feel at Church, what happens the first time they feel a lack of love? They fall away. Can you remember a time in your life when you didn't feel loved? You felt lonely, sorry for yourself, maybe even physically sick. But when we are rooted in Christ and His love, we are rooted in something solid and secure, because Christ's love never changes; it's always there. The love of our Heavenly Father is the same.

The Book of Mormon plays a crucial role in rooting people to Christ. Every aspect of a person's testimony is anchored in place by the Book of Mormon. Think of that: every aspect of a person's testimony is held in place by what is found in the pages of the Book of Mormon.

If you teach your investigators the Book of Mormon, you teach nothing but the gospel of Jesus Christ. If you teach the gospel of Christ with power, you will root them to Christ. If you root them to Christ, you will root them to the Atonement. If you root them to the Atonement, you will root them to the gospel. If you root them to the gospel, you will root them to faith, repentance, baptism, covenant making, and the gift of the Holy Ghost.

The degree to which we effectively help people understand how the Book of Mormon fulfills the Lord's divine purposes, is the same degree to which we will see them become convinced that Joseph Smith was a prophet. That's the same degree to which they will be committed to continual prayer and study of the Book of Mormon. And soon they will see that the Book of Mormon does lead them to Christ. So you can see the purpose and power of the Book of Mormon, the keystone of our religion.

FEASTING ON THE WORD OF GOD

Remember that before our investigators can sense the power and divinity of the Book of Mormon for themselves, they must sense it in us. We must delight in the word of God. We must love the Book of Mormon. We must feast upon its words.

When the Book of Mormon becomes delicious to you, you will sparkle. You will be excited. You'll visit your investigators and say, "Oh, I just had to drop by and read you this part here; this is so good I can hardly wait to tell you!" If you don't feel that way, your investigators won't feel that way. Now perhaps you can begin to understand why one precious half hour every day is spent supping from the pages of this book of books. Learn to love the book, and you'll not only love to live its teachings yourself, but you'll love to teach it.

President Benson said, "I would particularly urge you to read again and again the Book of Mormon and ponder and apply its teachings" ("Youth of the Noble Birthright," *Ensign*, May 1986, 43). Isn't that interesting? Ponder and apply its teachings. I try to do that every day, pondering the scriptures every night and then applying a scripture in my life every day. This daily application of scriptures can absolutely change our lives.

I taught the Book of Mormon for twenty-seven years, and I was always astounded when I would talk about something in class and a student would observe, "Oh, I read that once."

"Well," I said, "I teach this book every year and find things I've never even noticed before. The book is so full of truths it takes a lifetime of study to take it all in."

So, we had an assignment. I gave extra credit to students who read 2 Nephi 9 or Enos for thirty days in a row before going to bed. A student once asked me: "Why? Why do we need to read it every day? I mean, I'll get it after just a night or two."

"You just read it and see," is all I answered.

Well, one day I was walking to class, and all of a sudden this young man was waiting for me by the door. He literally leapt upon me, gave me a hug and said, "Oh, Brother Ed, Brother Ed, it's true, it's true!"

I said, "I know it's true, Elder."

"I understand what you mean now," he said. "I read Enos, and on the twenty-first day something happened inside. I wanted everybody to be converted. Brother Ed, I'm thinking of checking out of school and going on my mission today."

"Can't you just wait two more weeks until the semester ends?" I asked.

This young man fell in love with the Book of Mormon because he did what the Prophet said, again and again and again, and then he applied it in his life. Until we apply it to our lives, we will not delight in it. We will not enjoy this feeling. We will not be enthusiastic about it. But when we love it, we'll live it because we apply it.

Nephi understood this principle: "For my soul delighteth in the scriptures, and my heart pondereth them" (2 Ne. 4:15). President Benson also understood: "Reread the Book of Mormon so that we might more fully come to Christ, be committed to Him, centered in Him, and consumed in Him" (General Conference, October 1987).

Do you see now what will happen with your investigators? When Christ comes into our lives, we are born of God, and we'll also be strengthened through the Book of Mormon. If we are conscientious in our study of the Book of Mormon, we will not be susceptible to Satan's enticings. I promise you that if you'll earnestly and prayerfully ponder, and steadfastly read the Book of Mormon and live it, the adversary will have no effect upon you. And unless you do that, you will not be strong.

Why is this? How do we become spiritually strong? How do we grow in faith? The answer is always the same: the word of God applied in our lives makes us strong. It makes our spirits strong. In other words, when we delight, those we teach will be delighted. Every day we should have a goal to place a certain number of copies of the Book of Mormon. You'll begin to see the importance of the book and the role it plays in call backs and other teaching appointments.

Use the Book of Mormon to effectively get people to listen to your message. Ask them, "If you knew there was another book written that talked about Jesus Christ and what He did, would you like to read that? You would? Well, I just happen to have five copies of that very book right here in my pocket."

Have faith in the power of this book. If we believe that the Lord will prepare a way for people to accept our message, it will happen. Pray for the power of discernment to be led to those who would hear you. If we doubt it, I promise you it will not happen, and we will have a difficult time finding investigators. But if we believe with faith that the Book of Mormon will bring people unto Christ and that we can baptize, then it will happen.

HELPING INVESTIGATORS TO KNOW

When you place a copy of the Book of Mormon, the investigators need to feel your love so that you can all feel the Spirit. And after you've placed the book, always quietly pray in your heart and mind, "Is there something from the Book of Mormon that I could share with them that would touch their heart to bring them closer to God?" This needs to be in our minds every moment of every day. We never take that out of our minds. We never replace it with anything. Is there something from the Book of Mormon I could share with them that would cause them to want to change?

Of course, we first get a promise from them to read the book, and then we must schedule a follow-up visit. If we fail to get a follow-up visit, and then if we fail to follow up on the reading assignment, our investigators begin to think, "Don't tell me how much you want me to read this book. You asked me to read 1 Nephi 3:7, but you didn't even ask me the next time when you came whether I'd read it or not. And I stayed up late after bowling to read it! But you don't even care whether I read it or not."

When you mark those scriptures for your investigators to read, write it in your planner: "Friday 7 PM, Anderson Family (1 Nephi 3:7 and all of 2 Nephi 9)." You can even write notes about why you made particular assignments: "They were interested in the Atonement of Christ, so we invited them to read 2 Nephi 9 and Alma 40. They also were very interested in faith, so we assigned Moroni 7. And of course we had them read Moroni 10:3–5."

Now we've placed the book and we're faithfully following up on reading assignments. Next, we must teach investigators what they must do in order to qualify themselves to know that it's true.

Many missionaries tell their investigators, "Pray about the Book of Mormon and you can know if it's true or not." But they leave out a crucial step. Our investigators must qualify themselves to receive an answer from the Lord. They must study and pray, and then the Lord will tell them it's true.

This is how we help them qualify themselves. First, we ourselves must establish a pattern of reading the Book of Mormon regularly. We must have a special feeling about the book. We must have a clear understanding about Moroni 10:3–5 and explain that passage to our investigators in detail when we introduce the book.

We need to explain to them that when they're reading is when the Lord will testify to them it's true. They don't read all 531 pages and then say, "OK, I've finished reading. Now I pray." It's an ongoing daily process to know that the Book of Mormon is true. Make sure investigators understand that they don't need to wait until they've finished reading to start asking! To help them understand that, read through Moroni 10:3–5 with them, discussing specifically the following things: how the hand of God brought the book forward originally; how it was prepared by the prophets; how it came forth through Joseph Smith; and how it might be possible that the Lord has prepared them to find the Book of Mormon.

When investigators begin to read the book, they rehearse what they've learned—how merciful the Lord is, how he's been involved in the affairs of the people, what the prophets have done, etc. As they read, investigators will remember these things; they are then prepared to feel good as they read. Then we can explain to them that all good comes from a loving Heavenly Father and His beloved Son, Jesus Christ (see Moroni 7:16–17).

If our investigators are sincere after we've carefully followed these steps, things will begin to happen. They will ponder and pray about the contents of the Book of Mormon, and its teachings will become important in their lives. When Parley P. Pratt received the Book of Mormon he said that he couldn't eat or sleep; all he wanted to do was read the book. Parley P. Pratt was sincere, and so was qualified to receive an answer from the Lord. If our investigators are sincere, they'll ponder the contents of the Book of Mormon, and by means of the Spirit they will agree with the teachings.

In Galatians 5:22 we read: "But the fruit of the Spirit is love, joy, peace, longsuffering, gentleness, goodness, faith." When our investigators feel these things as they read the Book of Mormon, they'll recognize the Spirit and know that the book is true. Sometimes our investigators are unfamiliar with the Spirit, and they need a little help identifying where these wonderful feelings come from.

"How do you feel when you read the Book of Mormon?" you might ask them.

"Good," they'll answer.

"All good comes from our Heavenly Father," you'll teach. "And those feelings are a witness that the Book of Mormon is true."

One good thing about the teachings in the Book of Mormon is that they are also logical and rational; and they correspond with the Bible in many ways. We can use that as we teach investigators who are familiar with the Bible. But more important than that, are the things that the Spirit will cause our investigators to feel as they read: they'll understand the glorious truths; they'll recognize particular doctrines; and they'll know that it's uplifting and inspired. We must not fail to teach our investigators to recognize the witness of the Spirit.

Have you ever taught, or been with someone when they have taught, about a gospel principle, and the investigator says, "Well, that's what I've always believed"? But when you ask them what church they belong to, you discover that particular church doesn't even teach the principle in question.

So how could they possibly believe in that principle? Because we all came to this earth with the Light of Christ. And when we hear it repeated here, our heart resonates to it. The elect of God hear these teachings, and they find the teachings appealing. They experience a spiritual uplift.

One of the greatest truths we'll ever teach people is that they are children of God the Father, and that He has a plan that provides us eternal life and happiness. This is fundamental to the gospel of Jesus Christ and is taught in the first discussions. So many people in the world don't even realize this. And when we teach this to people and they pray about it, the Lord will tell them it's true; they'll receive answers and know that the doctrine is right.

Investigators tend to seek a sign when they are praying about the Book of Mormon. They want lights to go on three times in succession, or receive a visitation from an angel or something like that. We must not look for incredible signs when we're seeking to discover truth, but we must recognize the signs from the Spirit. That's why we, along with our investigators, must understand the true fruits of the Spirit (see Galatians 5:22).

The Spirit is the key. We must preach with love and concern, tenderly, and, as Alma counseled his sons, with soberness—then it will be easier to have the Spirit. Do not contend, and do not Bible-bash. Simply teach the Book of Mormon. There are more than two hundred different sects in the world today that believe the Bible. Preach from the book that was brought forth for our dispensation, and let the Spirit bear witness of that book. Then the Spirit can also bear witness to the truthfulness of the Bible, as far as it is translated correctly. But the truthfulness of the Book of Mormon is the key, and we must help our investigators gain that knowledge.

CONCLUSION

I bear witness that the gospel of Jesus Christ is true. The Book of Mormon is the Lord's book—the book for our time, to bless His children today. We must learn to use it on a daily basis with everyone we teach. If we do that, I know the Lord will bless us. The greatest tool we have to bring people unto Christ is the Book of Mormon.

⸙ 𝒞HAPTER 11 ⸙

TEACHING BY THE SPIRIT

Understanding our divine nature brings self-esteem, self-worth, and self-respect. We are the children of Heavenly Father, and so is everyone else in the rest of the world. This knowledge brings with it a desire to serve and bless our fellowmen. A desire to teach all mankind the gospel of Jesus Christ. To teach by the Spirit that they might come to know God and Jesus Christ and partake of their goodness.

RECOGNIZE HEAVENLY FATHER'S CHILDREN—AND THEY WILL RECOGNIZE THEMSELVES

I was at the hospital a few days ago, smiling at everyone I passed in the halls, when I realized that each one of them was one of Heavenly Father's children. Then I realized that there are more than five billion children of Heavenly Father on this earth, and that there have probably been that many before now, and for all I know, there may even be five billion yet to come. I wondered how righteous people should feel about Heavenly Father's children. Then I thought of Ammon and Omner and Himni and Aaron (they were righteous after they repented, as all of us become righteous after we repent) and how they felt about Heavenly Father's children.

In Mosiah 28:3, the sons of Mosiah had just talked to their father, King Mosiah, who was a very great man (his best friend was Alma the prophet, so he must have been a great man). They said, "Dad, could we please go to the Lamanites and preach?"

Those Nephites with minimum mentality probably wondered, "Why would you want to work with those savages who are trying to kill us?" But this is what the sons of Mosiah thought:

> They were desirous that salvation should be declared to every creature, for they could not bear that any human soul should perish; yea, even the very thoughts that any soul should endure endless torment did cause them to quake and tremble (Mosiah 28:3).

Now, if you apply the Atonement to your lives, then you'll taste His love and want that privilege for the investigators you teach. This is the most incredible thing you will ever see in conversion: when the power and love of God is placed in an anointed servant of God, and that servant teaches the worth of souls to those honest in heart. You can watch those people change before your very eyes. All of a sudden, their eyes will start to light up. They'll say, "Oh yes, I see, tell me more!" And in this process of enlightenment, guess what they receive? The gift of self-esteem. They recognize where they came from—"I am a child of God and I now understand His plan for me, and I want it. I want to be baptized."

Some of you might say, "Oh President, you make it sound like it's so easy." I know that it's tough, but trust in the Lord and don't ever let fear conquer you. I don't want any of you to fear. I have seen every sin you could imagine and every mortal punishment of that sin, as well as the change that comes into the lives of people who accept the gospel. I have seen alcoholics, atheists, and derelicts reborn as they remember who they are and where they come from. And your desire to be able to give this gift of knowledge should overcome all your fear.

DESIRE TO LOVE YOUR FELLOWMEN THAT YOU MAY TEACH THEM

Did the sons of Mosiah have the love of God in their hearts? Did they have the love of Christ in their hearts? Even the very *thought* that any human soul would be in the telestial kingdom, or any place unsuitable for Heavenly Father's children, caused them to tremble and quake. Think of how you feel when someone you love is sick. You've all prayed for brothers and sisters, cousins or aunts, grandmas and grandpas, fathers and mothers, right? "Oh Father, please let them live! Oh, don't let them die!" We plead for mortality like it's the end of the earth.

If I were to run to you in a panic and say, "Come quick! Tricia Pinegar [my daughter] is lost up in the mountains. She's lost! My baby!" I wouldn't even doubt that you would come and help me. I know you'd come because you enjoy helping people who need help. It's interesting that we will pass by those who don't appear to need help, but we will quickly run to help others whose need is more obvious. Until you love others and until you desire the welfare of their souls, you will never teach people with sufficient power to bring them to a knowledge of Christ. That is what I want to teach you: to preach and teach with power. So begin by desiring to love your fellowmen enough that you will be able to teach them with the Spirit, that you might bring souls to Christ.

THE POWER OF THE SPIRIT CARRIES THE MESSAGE TO THEIR HEARTS

With that desire starting to kindle in our souls, we can do anything. If our investigators want to stop receiving the discussions, we'll say, "Oh please, won't you listen one more time?" They often won't listen until they see your true concern, but when they see and feel your concern for them, you will have the power to awaken their souls to God. You will have savor. Do you know what savor is? In D&C 101:39-40, we read: "When men [and women] are called unto mine everlasting gospel, and covenant with an everlasting covenant [and we've done that], they are accounted as the salt of the earth and the savor of men; They are called to be the savor of men; therefore, if that salt [you and me] of the earth lose its savor, behold, it is thenceforth good for nothing only to be cast out and trodden under the feet of men." In other words, to be "the salt of the earth" and "the savor of men" means to have the power to awaken people to God. But if we don't desire to do this, we'll lose our savor and never have this power and influence.

When you have the salt within you and the savor is in your soul, the Spirit will do its part, as Nephi tells, that if you have this desire, despite your weaknesses, the power of the Spirit will carry it into the hearts of your investigators and the less active members you meet (2 Ne. 33:1).

OBTAIN THE WORD

When you care enough for the people you're teaching, and you have the desire to do your best, the Lord will put into your heart and bring to your lips the things you should say at the very moment that you need them. When you have this desire, you are willing to pay the price to gain the knowledge to teach. Do you recall the Lord's words in D&C 11? "First seek to obtain my word, and then shall your tongue be loosed" (D&C 11:21). That's why you are here, to obtain the word. Then you will be given the power. If you just go out in the field and say, "Oh Heavenly Father, I haven't searched the scriptures, I haven't learned my discussions, but I'm a nice guy and I'm out here, give me the words," you'll find yourself saying, "I can't understand why that discussion didn't go very well."

Do you remember what was happening about the time of Alma 17:2–3? Alma had gone one way and the sons of Mosiah had gone another way, and they met up again as the sons of Mosiah were traveling toward the land of Zarahemla. Alma must have said something like, "Oh Ammon, Omner, Himni, and Aaron, it's so good to see you," and no doubt they exchanged embraces and hugs. Then Alma said that what added to his joy was that his friends had "waxed strong in the knowledge of the truth" and that "they were men of a sound understanding." Why? Because "they had searched the scriptures diligently, that they might know the word of God."

For missionaries in the field, the hours between 7:30 and 9:30 in the morning are gospel study time and companion study time, when you role-play and study so you might also know the word of God. Many missionaries don't do that properly. The Lord says, "I, the Lord, am bound when ye do what I say; but when ye do not what I say, ye have no promise" (D&C 82:10). And D&C 130:20 states that all blessings are predicated upon laws we must obey. If you don't study to obtain the knowledge, the Lord will not automatically give it to you and bring it to your memory in tough situations.

THE LORD IS IN CHARGE

In 1 Nephi 4:6, Nephi said, "And I was led by the Spirit, not knowing beforehand the things which I should do." That didn't mean that Nephi hadn't studied or prayed or worked. He had already been righteous up to this point. But at that moment he didn't know what to do. You will probably have the same thing happen to you out in the field. You'll say, "Oh Father," and at that moment when you pray, "What should I do?" then all of a sudden the words will come. You'll find yourself saying, "And by the power of the Spirit, I testify to you, Mr. Brown, that what I have said is true, and I know it's true because the Lord bore witness to me that it's true." You will bear your testimony with power, and then you'll wonder, "How did I do that?" Remember, the Lord is in charge!

When you teach with power, you teach the mind and the will of God. You fulfill Doctrine and Covenants 68:4; you speak by the Spirit, and the Spirit speaks the word of Christ, which is the mind and the will of God.

DON'T EAT YOUR SPIRITUAL FEAST INTRAVENOUSLY

Have you ever pureed anything? That's where you take the blender and chop something up at a very high speed. Have you ever pureed a filet mignon and then drunk it? Doesn't that sound stupid? Who in their right mind would take a filet mignon, medium rare, and say, "Well, it's time for a filet, great!" and toss it in the blender. You wouldn't do that! You'd take a knife and fork, and you'd slice the meat, and you'd put it in your mouth and begin to chew. You might even roll your eyes back, savoring that bite, and in your heart thank Heavenly Father for food. (Ooh, I can taste it right now!) And you would chew it slowly so you could enjoy it. You would smile between each bite, each chew.

That's the way you need to read the scriptures. You don't speed through like you're on a bullet bike. You don't say, "Oh yeah, I read the Book of Mormon" while you're thoughtfully tapping your finger on your chin, trying to remember when that happened. You don't say, "Oh yeah, I took a speed-reading class and I can speed-read an entire chapter in five seconds." That's like getting food through intravenous feedings. You'd get just barely enough to stay alive!

Now, do you think Ammon, Omner, Himni, and Aaron were entitled to any more of the Spirit of the Lord than we are? You'd better not, because they weren't. They had to "search the scriptures diligently" (Alma 17:2–3) just like we do. Every story you read in the Book of Mormon (except for the 12,000 converts and the four-teen-year missions) can be duplicated in every mission of the Church today. The biggest miracle in the world is conversion, and the missionaries who have this great converting power are the missionaries who pay the price. But if you set your study aside, supposing that you know of yourselves, or thinking that you can wing it or just take it easy, you'll be the missionary who says, "Why is this so hard? My momma didn't tell me it'd be like this. President, I want to go home. I'm not having any fun. Other missionaries told me this would be the happiest two years of my life, and I don't feel much happiness."

I'll tell you something. I certainly knew a lot of happy mission-aries, because they worked and they studied as hard as they could. They were men and women of sound understanding, and they did wax strong in the knowledge of truth because they had gained this knowledge through diligent work and study.

This knowledge comes through searching the scriptures and good books. I had the joy and the privilege of teaching the Book of

Mormon for a long time—about twenty-seven years. That's eight years more than most elders have been alive! I studied and I taught that book. Oh, how I love that book! Last December, I realized that my old scriptures were crinkled and the back was broken. I'd used the Book of Mormon so much, it just turned open to the Book of Mormon and the Doctrine and Covenants automatically. So I decided that I deserved some new scriptures, and I bought two sets: a set that I carry around with me and a large set that sits on my desk.

I read the New Testament, the Book of Mormon, the Doctrine and Covenants, and Pearl of Great Price, and I marked all of the Book of Mormon, Doctrine and Covenants, and all of the New Testament. I didn't just read the books; I feasted upon the words, intensely searched them, and pondered them. Then I would underline and apply a particular scripture to my life. So when I read, I had to go slowly.

After that I went to my wife and said, "Sweetheart, I don't know what's wrong with me."

"What's the matter, honey?" she asked.

I answered, "I just finished the Book of Mormon again and it's like I read it for the first time."

She said, "What do you mean?" I said, "I've never learned so much in my life!" So I prayed and I said, "Father, why? Why am I just learning this now? Why did I learn so much more this time than the last twenty-five times?"

And the answer was, "My son, you were a good boy before and you're still OK, but you see, you read it this time with a different purpose in mind. The last time you read, you were just reading for a little knowledge for a class—like it's just part of the job, something you do because you have to. This time your mind isn't thinking of anything except how you can bless Heavenly Father's children. You are totally consumed with how you can use the book, how you can live the book, and how you can bless lives every minute."

Do you know the beautiful part about a mission? The only thing that you do is missionary work. You go to sleep and you wake up and you do missionary work. And elders (Hallelujah!) don't have to think about girls or dates or ask, "What'll we do tonight, where shall we go?" You don't have to think about any of those things! All you do is eat, drink, and sleep the scriptures, pray and ponder, and ask how you can bless Heavenly Father's children so they'll come to Christ.

Here is a little parable for you. A rich young nobleman (let's call him Elder Milligan) walked up to Socrates and said, "Socrates, you are so smart." Socrates was a little embarrassed and blustered around a bit modestly, and Elder Milligan continued, "I would like you to teach me all that you know."

Socrates said, "You bet I will, I'll teach you. I'll give you all of my knowledge." He invited Elder Milligan down to the river, and they hiked down the path together. When they got to the river, they walked into the water until they were about up to their chests and old Socrates said, "Look up there." The rich young nobleman looked up, and as he did so, Socrates (who was unusually strong) pushed him under the water and held him there. Elder Milligan tried to get up but Socrates wouldn't let him. As Elder Milligan struggled to break out of the old man's grip, he felt the air leak out of his lungs until there wasn't any air left. Just when he decided he was about to drown, Socrates let him up and said, "When you want to learn as badly as you wanted to breathe, you come back and I'll teach you all I know."

My point is, that until you have an insatiable desire to gain the knowledge you need, to know your discussions, to know how to find people, and to be able to build relationships of trust, you will never be able to teach with power. How does the Lord teach that same thing in the Beatitudes? He said, "Blessed are all they who do hunger and thirst after righteousness, for they shall be filled with the Holy Ghost" (3 Ne. 12:6). If you want to learn, if you care about these people, then pay the price to learn. Get that knowledge.

PURIFY OURSELVES AND REMEMBER WHOSE HANDS WE ARE

So, we've got the desire and we have the knowledge, or we're working on the knowledge. Now we need to purify ourselves. Do you ever wonder why some missionaries can't do things that others can do? Why some people can perform miracles that other people can't? In 3 Nephi we read: "And there was not any man who could do a miracle in the name of Jesus save he were cleansed every whit from his iniquity" (3 Ne. 8:1). Now, if you'd like to, cross reference that to D&C 76:69, which teaches us, "These are they who are just men made perfect." They are the ones who enter the celestial kingdom.

Do you want to be a just person and see miracles happen in your mission? We read how in Moroni. We're told that angels cease to come only because people lack faith (Moroni 7:37). If you have faith, what happens? You repent, just like Enos did. He asked, "Why am I free of this guilt, Father?" And He was answered, "Because of thy *faith* in Christ, whom thou hast never before heard nor seen" (Enos 1:8).

What is required of us in order to be cleansed from iniquity? Fifty-five thousand years of righteousness? No, just honest repentance. This is the key: if you do something wrong, repent. Don't muck in the mire, don't live in the past. Repent. You will also see how incredibly happy people are when they finally realize that they can repent, and you will watch the light come into their eyes because of what you've given them—the knowledge that they can repent.

When we repent in righteousness through confession and forsaking, and through good works, we become sanctified. We become holy and pure, without spot, so the Lord can work with us. That's why repentance is a daily ritual. Do you know what happens as we become purified? We become worthy instruments.

We learn about "worthy instruments" in Alma 29:9. Alma said:

> I know that which the Lord hath commanded me [now remember to apply this scripture to yourself], and I glory in it. I do not glory of myself, but I glory in that which the Lord hath commanded me; yea, and this is my glory, that perhaps I may be an instrument in the hands of God to bring some soul to repentance; and this is my joy.

Purity and purification make you an instrument in the hands of the Lord, and the Lord will use us if we desire it in our hearts and if we're trying to be purified.

You might say, "President Pinegar, that's the trouble! You quote from Alma here, and you quote from Enos there, and they're free from iniquity. You want me to be like them, and you forget who I am." No, that's not the trouble. You've forgotten who *you* are. You are instruments in the Lord's hand just as any of the prophets are. All the missionaries of the Lord have power to call down angels. That's part of the power of faith which you elders and sisters have access to. Purify yourselves, and sit back and watch the miracles in your mission.

ACQUIRING FAITH

Now, let's think of some personal things we must do that involve our faith, our attributes, and our skills. First of all, you will teach with power no faster than you grow in faith, because faith is the foundation of all righteousness.

Spencer W. Kimball, Ezra Taft Benson, and Marion G. Romney (who was in the First Presidency at one time) gave us four ways to acquire faith. We can also increase our faith in other ways, but these are the primary ones: searching the scriptures, prayer and fasting, being righteous, and building up the kingdom.

Search the Scriptures

Isn't it interesting that we're given the same formula to acquire the Spirit that we use to grow stronger in love and faith? Having the love of God, the Spirit, and faith, all require the same four things. Searching the scriptures, the word of God, is the only way you can have faith. That's based on Romans 10:17: "So then faith cometh by hearing, and hearing by the word of God."

Prayer and Fasting

The second step President Benson taught, is to acquire faith through fasting and prayer. Now think of Helaman 3:35 and Alma 17:3, where they waxed stronger in faith through fasting and prayer. Fasting + prayer = faith. When we fast and pray, we will also be filled with love, just as it says in Moroni 7:48, that if we pray with all the energy of our hearts, we will be filled with the love of Christ, that we might preach the gospel and share it with our fellowmen.

Be Righteous

The third step is acquiring personal righteousness. Righteousness comes from obedience—and that will give you the Spirit. We covenant each week, as we partake of the sacrament, to keep the commandments, to be obedient. The blessing associated with this is that the Lord promises that we can always have His Spirit to be with us (see D&C 20:77, 79). Faith is a gift of the Spirit (see 1 Cor. 12:9). We know that the gifts of the Spirit are predicated upon righteousness, and given to those who love God and keep the commandments (see D&C 46:9).

Build up the Kingdom

The fourth way to acquire faith is through building up the kingdom. You can be righteous by doing many things, but you are especially so when you're anxiously engaged in building up the kingdom. Faith is not only acquired, but strengthened by building up the kingdom of God. Faith is active whether we are hoping, working, or exercising its power. Therefore, as we seek to build up the kingdom by bringing souls to Christ, our faith increases. Just as bearing a testimony strengthens a testimony, likewise, when we do faith-promoting things our faith is increased (see Hebrews 11; Alma 32; Ether 12; Moroni 7).

Faith is a multidimensional principle. Truly our faith increases with hearing the word of God, praying and fasting, living righteously, receiving the gifts of the Spirit, and building up the kingdom of God. Faith is enhanced throughout our lives. Whether we're looking at the creations of God, or seeing the good in mankind, we can increase our faith continually. And most importantly for our missions, as our faith increases we have the power to teach by the Spirit.

CONCLUSION

As you build and strengthen your faith, increase your love of Christ, wax strong in the knowledge of the truth, you will grow in confidence. You will be able to stand and give your first discussion with power and love. And if some of you forget something, don't worry. If you do it with love, people will understand. But you'll become so good once you have the Spirit that nothing can stop you. Your investigators and converts will call you blessed. And the day will come when Heavenly Father will thank you and say, "Well done, good and faithful servant; thou hast been faithful over a few things, I will make thee ruler over many things" (Matthew 25:23).

CHAPTER 12

HELPING THEM RECOGNIZE THE SPIRIT: GETTING COMMITMENTS

When we teach with power and authority, we are filled with charity. We speak by the Spirit and have the power, through faith, of convincing our fellowmen that what we say is true (see Alma 62:45). When, with faith, you have that kind of power and authority, you are able to help people make and keep commitments.

RECOGNIZING AND USING THE SPIRIT

People can feel the Spirit all of their life, but until they recognize and identify it, they will not know its source, or the good that it can cause in their lives when they act upon those promptings to do good. Once they feel the Spirit, and you ask, "How do you feel when we teach you these things?" or "How did you feel when you read the Book of Mormon?" or "How did you feel when you attended Church?"; they respond by saying, "I feel love, peace, joy, long suffering, gentleness, goodness, faith, meekness and temperance" (see Galatians 5:22–23), or "I had a desire to do good, to do justly, to walk humbly. My mind was enlightened. I made good judgment. I felt joy" (see D&C 11:12–13). These are the feelings of the Spirit. And when someone feels the Spirit, then we invite them to make and keep a commitment.

It is imperative that when investigators feel the Spirit, we are sensitive enough to identify it and help them recognize it; then we can ask them to make a commitment. The words you will use to help them make those commitments are *"will you."* For example, "Will you read the Book of Mormon? Will you pray about the Church? Will you pray about Joseph being the prophet of the Restoration? Will you pray about the truthfulness of the Book of Mormon? Will you pray for strength to keep the word of wisdom?" The words "*will you*" are the key to helping people make and keep commitments; and people change and are converted no faster than they make and keep those commitments.

I promised the elders in the mission, if you get more than five investigators past the third discussion, I will come any night, every night of my life in England, and teach—give a fireside or a cottage meeting. Well, the elders in the Guilford ward had five. They called me up, "President we've got five."

I still remember my talk; it was on 2 Peter—taking upon yourself the divine nature of Christ (1:3–12). After the talk, I walked down and started to visit with the investigators. I said, "Debbie, it's so good to be with you, and I'm so glad that you were here tonight. It was nice to meet you."

I said, "How did you feel?"

She said, "Oh it's so good."

I said, "Well, how do you feel when the elders teach you?"

"Oh, I just want to be good."

I said, "You know that's the Spirit?"

She said, "Yes I love going to church."

I said, "How do you feel about the Book of Mormon?"

"Oh, I love to read it."

I asked, "How do you feel about its truthfulness?"

"Oh I know it's true." And then all of a sudden the Spirit spoke to me, and said that she was ready.

I said, "Debbie, you know this week I'm fairly busy, but on Thursday night I have some time. *Will you* be baptized Thursday night?"

She said, "Why yes President, I'd be glad to be baptized. Will you baptize me?"

I answered excitedly, "Oh Debbie, I'll be glad to baptize you." She felt the Spirit so she was willing to commit.

Then Debbie told me that Sister Chote and Brother Chote had been coming along quite nicely. So I said to Sister Chote, "Debbie mentioned that you've enjoyed the missionaries."

"Oh yes, I love the Book of Mormon, I love going to church."

Then I asked her, "Sister Chote, then you felt that feeling of wanting to do good and follow Christ, and when you come to know that these things are true, do you want to follow Christ and be baptized?"

"Oh yes, I feel that way President Pinegar."

At that point I told her about Debbie being baptized on Thursday night and asked her if she would be willing to be baptized Thursday night as well. She said, "Why yes, I would love to. Will you baptize me?"

I told her I'd be tickled to do that. But then she told me that Brother Chote was having a little trouble with tithing. So I spoke to Brother Chote. "Brother Chote, your beautiful wife has mentioned that she's excited and wants to be baptized Thursday. She mentioned that you struggle a little bit with the principle of tithing."

He responded, "Well, yes."

Then I said, "Brother Chote, I want to bear you my testimony. I promise you that if you pay your tithing, because you know that this Church is true, I promise you that your finances will be OK, and things will work out, and the Lord will bless you. If you will make and keep this commitment, you can covenant with the Lord and come into His Church."

He said, "President Pinegar, I'll be baptized."

Well now I was just on cloud nine. They were having squash and biscuits (that's punch and cookies in England), so I walked up and asked the elders if they thought they could work out a baptism for Thursday.

And they asked, "Oh, who's being baptized?" When I told them it was Debbie and Brother and Sister Chote, they wanted to know how I knew that; and who had asked them.

I said, "I did. Is that OK?"

"Well how did you do that?"

So I told them. "I simply asked, 'Will you be baptized?' and they said 'yes,' because they felt the Spirit." The baptisms were wonderful. The bishop and the home teachers and visiting teachers were there. It was wonderful!

Sometimes we're so afraid to make the invitation for commitment that we stop the progression of the investigators. If you're not afraid to ask them to make a commitment, you can have great success. What's the worst thing that could happen if you ask them to come to church? They'll say "No"?

OK? I mean, no one was killed, no one died, they just said they couldn't come to church. For all you know, they were going out of town that week.

Sometimes we're so afraid. We wait for a great manifestation like a burning bush, or the writing on the wall. Ask for the commitment! I would tell all the elders and sisters that in every discussion they should ask people to make and keep a commitment, then investigators have a chance to grow. When you get old and become a mother or a father, that's how you'll get your children to clean their rooms. "Will you clean your room? How do you feel about living in our house?"

"Oh I love you Mom, I love you Dad."

"Then will you clean your room?" The fact is, people change when they feel your love and make and keep commitments.

One time the elders said, "President, we've got this couple, they're the greatest. Could you meet us at the visitors' center?" I told them I'd be glad to. I went to the visitors' center to meet the couple.

The senior companion came up to me and said, "President, we've been working with these people about five or six weeks now, and they've heard all the discussions. They've been to church a couple of times and we're really thinking they're good, but, kind of, well . . . don't come on too strong."

I looked at the elder and said, "Elder, do you want the Spirit to help us?"

He got a little nervous and realized what he was doing. I went up to the couple and I said, "The elders have written to me about you. You are wonderful. They love you so much. They care about your happiness so much. You know, sometimes we get nervous when we teach the lessons for fear we might offend people. You know they wouldn't offend you for the world. Tell me, how do you feel about the Church, the Book of Mormon, the Prophet Joseph?"

And they said, "Oh, wonderful!" and they just answered "yes" to everything. They were the elect of the Lord.

And I said, "You know, I'm coming down to Salsbury a week from today; I sure would love to come to your baptism. *Will you* be baptized on that day?"

"Of course, President, we'd be tickled. Hey elders, we're going to be baptized next Sunday night. Is that OK? Is that all right with you?"

The elder looked at me like, "How did you do that?"

And then I said, "I just asked." Fear flees when we have the courage to invite people. Don't ever let fear stop the process.

Rather than fearing to offend, help them recognize the Spirit and its power in their lives. When people are doing what's right, and they feel a good feeling, encourage them not to expect something more or greater or bigger. To feel peace, to feel joy, to have a desire to be nice—these are the feelings of the Spirit. Witness to them the value of their commitment through the good feelings they have about what they're doing. Often people want more or bigger feelings. The young brother I just baptized said, "I've always felt good about it, but I want to really, really, really know." And then I said, "Oliver Cowdery had a problem like this once. And in D&C 6:23 the Lord said, "[Oliver,] did I not speak peace to your mind . . . What greater witness can you have than from God?" And when you witness that those feelings are the Spirit, then they will know that what they are doing is good. And when they understand and recognize the whisperings of the Spirit, it will help them make and keep their commitments.

INVOKING THE SPIRIT

So, to help people make commitments, number one, be sure they feel the Spirit. They must understand that their good feelings are testifying to their heart that your teachings are true. The things that they read and ponder are true. Once they feel the Spirit, you identify it as the Spirit and help them recognize it as such. Then you can invite them to make and keep a commitment.

All this growth and desire for committing begins when we teach by the Spirit. In D&C 50:17–22 it talks about when we teach by the Spirit of truth, and when others hear it by the Spirit of truth, both are edified, and both are lifted, and both grow. As the Spirit is felt, then we can teach with power and move toward commitments. How do we do this? We must be personally worthy. We must be personally prepared. We must understand and appreciate the message, our role as elders and sisters—as messengers—and the worth of souls. If we love them, and we are worthy, we still need to help our investigators be worthy to feel the Spirit. We need to invoke the Spirit in our own lives and in their lives.

There are many ways to invoke the Spirit in your interactions with investigators. Take the time to read the Book of Mormon with your investigators. In our family we read the Book of Mormon out loud for years. I remember when the children first started; they thought I was a crazy, bald, senile, old man, and I probably was, but later they saw the value. As the younger children were born, they didn't know anything else but scripture time. I remember they became so excited to get their copies of the Book of Mormon with the gold letters on them, and their red pencils to underline. And when we read the Book of Mormon, we would read aloud. Tonight at ten o'clock I'll be propped up in bed with my wife and we'll read again out of the scriptures. Read the scriptures aloud with your contacts. This helps them feel the Spirit and desire to act on those good feelings.

Show them you love them. Assist them in every way, temporally and spiritually. If they're busy and they can't hear a discussion, and their boys are playing soccer, well, what should we do, elders and sisters? Let's go see the soccer game, of course. That's a great teaching moment. You are their friend and you care about what they care about. You can do all kinds of good things. But you let the families know that you love and care about them. Make regular contact, either in person, through a member, with a note, with a card, with a telephone call, with whatever it might be, and even drop off some chocolate chip cookies. Make regular contacts of love. When you contact people it means you care. When you make these regular contacts, it always reminds them, refreshes their memories, about the great commitments they are keeping.

Make church attendance high on the list in preparing your investigators for conversion and baptism. The more that people attend church, the more likely they'll be to make and keep all the commitments to become good members of the Church. Attending church introduces them to a support group who is trying to keep the same covenants and commitments. It also gives them more opportunities to feel the Spirit. This is wonderful, because the Spirit is the main governing thing that determines conversion and baptism, and gives people the continued desire to make and keep their commitments and covenants.

GIVE THEM P.I.E.

Another way to help our investigators and converts commit is to give them P.I.E. Now, I don't mean that we bribe them with an actual pie. P.I.E. is an acronym for *praise, instruct,* and *encourage.* These three steps apply to numerous situations. For example, always keep the commitments simple and measurable so you can respond to each step they take. Respond during the follow-up. Always, always arrange to follow up. It will tell them that you care and that you love them. When you're following up, always make sure you arrange for it in advance; never make it a surprise, because surprise follow-ups sometimes breed a lack of trust. So, back to our acronym; when following up: (1) **Praise** them—tell them how grateful you are that they are reading the Book of Mormon, that they're saying their prayers, or that they came to church; (2) **Instruct** them, specifically, about the things you want them to do; (3) and **Encourage** them to keep at it. That's the kind of P.I.E. we need to give them; we should praise, instruct, and encourage them. And when we do that, people are more willing to keep their commitments.

Here's an example. In our family, on the first family home evening after fast Sundays, we had family council. And during family council we counseled together and discussed ways we could be a happy family. I would have each child come up and stand by daddy and I would praise them and say, "We're so grateful for what's happened. Karie Lyn has done this, Steven's done this, Kelly's done this, Kristi's done this, Brett's done this, Cory's done this, Traci's done this, and Tricia's done this." Now my children are all in the book; they'll feel good. One time, when Cory was five, I asked my sweetheart, "What has Cory done lately?" She told me that he was in charge of putting away the dishes. He had committed to putting away the breakfast dishes every day. So I arranged for a follow-up to say, "Cory, the table is nice, you've done a good job." So I called Cory up. Now remember we're talking about *praise, instruct* and *encourage.* Cory came up, and he kept his commitment, so I said, "Kids, this is Cory Pinegar, the greatest 'dish-putter-awayer' on the entire planet earth." Cory smiled.

The week went on and my wife said, "Honey, you wouldn't believe it. Cory was perfect before; but now he's super perfect."

Every day he asks me, "Is this good enough, Mom? Do you want them set over here? What's the best . . .?" He was so committed because he had been praised, he'd been instructed, and he'd been encouraged. People keep commitments when you praise them honestly and genuinely. Instruct them about what to do; inform them of how good they are doing, and what it is they are feeling; and then encourage them to do better, or to keep up the good work. When you do this, they will feel a sense of achievement. They will feel a sense of accomplishment and success. This builds your relationship with them. Your mutual trust, respect, love, and your unity will all be stronger.

Be loving, yet bold. Alma told Shiblon to be bold but not overbearing. Be understanding and empathetic. Sometimes investigators may not keep their commitments. Don't threaten them and don't belittle them; but say, "I'm sorry you weren't able to do that; could we read today?" or "Would next week be better for church?" Let them know that you love them, and if there is ever a conflict, you let them know that your love is deeper than their inability to keep every commitment, because sometimes they just may not be at their best. Sometimes they just may make a mistake. When they've made their commitment and kept it, be supportive. Give genuine praise and encouragement

THE GENTLE REMINDER

Our constant love and encouragement should serve to remind our investigators of their commitments. But, even as we strive not to be overbearing, we must also directly ask them how they are doing. Always reconfirm the commitment and arrange for a follow-up. But don't forget, in the follow-up, the way we should remind our investigators of their responsibilities. I'll never forget when, as a young boy (it was in the olden days when we did ward teaching), all of a sudden out of the blue, the supervisor would call and ask, "Ed is your ward teaching done?"

I'd say, "No."

He'd say, "Why isn't your ward teaching done; it's the sixteenth of the month?"

And, well, I didn't know. And I'd think, *I didn't know you would call me today, and I'm just a senior in high school, and I'm studying now, and why do you call me? I don't want you to call me. I don't like you calling me.* You know why? Because he never arranged. I was just a kid. He never arranged and said, "Ed, you know the bishop really cares about this work. What would be the best day that you feel you could make the initial visit to your members and give them a little message? Would the third Sunday be OK? By the third Sunday could you do that?"

"Why yes, I could do that."

"Would it be all right if I called you up on the third Sunday to see how your people are feeling, and then I could report to the bishop about how well they are doing."

"That would be fine; that would be great." But he didn't do that. That's why I didn't like to go ward teaching as a boy, because I never did it on the right day. I mean, I didn't know the day he was going to call. I just wasn't ready. Arranging to follow up is vital in helping people make and keep their commitments.

Having others around to ask how they're doing is a wonderful plus. Another way to gently remind our investigators is to involve members of the ward as joint teachers, or let stake missionaries, or leaders of the ward (like the bishop or Relief Society president), go with you. It gives the investigators strength, especially if the investigator has a friend, or a friendshipper, in the ward who is close to them. A new convert especially works wonders in this capacity, because they have just gone through the process. This support helps them make and keep their commitments.

Another way to remind your investigators of why they should keep their commitments is to treat them like converts; take them with you to teach a first discussion. And they'll hear it again and say, "I remember I felt some of those feelings. I remember when they taught me that, I did . . ." and all of a sudden they are empowered, because they know they are doing good. Involve them as missionaries as you teach other investigators. Invite them to baptisms. Remember, always show love and concern, and assist them to make and keep commitments through gentle reminders.

RESOLVING CONCERNS THAT BLOCK THE SPIRIT

Often, when you ask investigators to make a commitment, you will uncover a concern that causes them not to feel the Spirit. If you ask them to make and keep a commitment and they say they can't, then you're in the process of discovering the concern. Then you help them, as you discuss the concern, to resolve it, so that they may want to come to church, or read the Book of Mormon, or be baptized. Remember, we only help people come into the Church *after* they have felt the Spirit and want to make and keep commitments.

What the Spirit does is help us baptize converts—converts to the Lord Jesus Christ. We must teach investigators that more than just feeling the Spirit is required to come unto Christ. Help them see the need for commitment, even commitment beyond baptism. As the Lord mentions, once we've entered in the way and made our commitment to be baptized, everything is not done. We must press forward with steadfastness (see 2 Ne. 31:19–21). We want people to stay committed to prepare to go to the temple. Commitment and covenants are important parts of enduring to the end.

One of the greatest ways you can help them alleviate their own self-doubt and desire to commit, is to find out their integrity level. As soon as possible you can say words like: "If you come to know that the things we teach you are true, will you be willing to follow Christ and be baptized?" So simple. Then we know if they really care about changing their life. Sometimes they might say no. Sometimes they might be nervous, or even scared, and it's OK. This kind of question helps people overcome fear, because learning for themselves becomes a challenge—that's why it's called the soft challenge. By using the soft challenge you can help people say, "Yes, when I know it is true, I would want to follow Christ and be baptized." Be a testifying, challenging, and committing missionary.

The Spirit dispels fear. One of the best ways to help your investigators overcome concerns is to feel the Spirit and gain a testimony of the gospel. So once again, have them read the Book of Mormon—this will help them feel the Spirit and gain a testimony despite their fears. If the Book of Mormon is true, and it is true, then Jesus is the Christ. If the Book of Mormon is true, and it is true, Joseph is the prophet of the Restoration. If the Book of Mormon is true, and it is true, the gospel has been restored. If the Book of Mormon is true, and it's true, this is the true Church. And if this is the true Church, it is led by a Prophet today. These facts make the Book of Mormon a powerful tool in the process of conversion and blessing the lives of those we teach. When you get people committed to read, study, and pray with the Book of Mormon as their guide, they are on the way to conversion.

The Book of Mormon saved my life and it saved my family. It converted me; it converted our family. The Book of Mormon has power. President Benson said the Book of Mormon is the great converter, because when people believe it is true, all concerns are washed away (in mission president's seminar, June 25, 1986). Can you see that if you want to teach with power and commitment, you must use the Book of Mormon? Always use it.

REMEMBERING OUR OWN COMMITMENTS

As missionaries, and as future parents in Zion, we must remember that we don't change any faster than we make and keep commitments. The Lord calls them covenants. Our exaltation is determined by how well we have kept our baptismal, our priesthood, and our temple covenants. And when we keep those covenants, the promises and blessings are ours. I have learned that when covenants are deepened because our commitment is strong, our lives are different. If in your lives—either at this moment as elders and sisters, or later—you find yourselves vacillating, look deep into your souls and check your level of commitment to your covenants. And when your level of commitment to your covenants has deepened to where you feel that it is life eternal to keep them, you will be a missionary for life. You will help many souls come unto Christ. When you make covenants with the Lord at that altar in the temple, and you become a mother or father, and find yourselves missionaries of a whole different sort, you will find that you'll never be totally converted until you learn to make and keep covenants by committing yourselves to the Lord.

CONCLUSION

Our blessings here and hereafter are dependent upon keeping the covenants we make with God. We re-covenant each week. This is how Heavenly Father helps us—by continually reminding us of our commitments to His law and His covenants. The Spirit will help us keep those covenants, and keeping those covenants will exalt us.

← CHAPTER 13 →

RECOGNIZING THE WORTH OF SOULS: ACTIVATION

The worth of souls is great in the sight of our God. We learn in John 15:16 that the Savior was praying that the apostles' fruit might remain—that is, that the Saints, after baptism, would be retained in the kingdom of God. The balanced effort in missionary work is this: we should simultaneously emphasize conversion, retention, and activation. In other words, just because people are baptized, doesn't mean the work is over. The work with them is forever. As missionaries, and as members, we are working together to help bring souls truly to Christ. After their baptism we should always help converts prepare for the temple to be sealed for time and all eternity, or prepare for their missions. We always let people know there's more to the kingdom than just being baptized. We want enduring conversions. Just being baptized is not enough. They have to acquire a deep and abiding testimony of the gospel of Jesus Christ and the Church. Most importantly, they must make a social transition in the Church. They must make friends—find a support group—so that they want to change their lifestyles, to abandon habits and activities that are inappropriate.

You see, people need to know that they're loved. People need to find joy within the Church and kingdom of God. Why is this important? Because, as President Hinckley has taught us, every one of Heavenly Father's children needs a friend, a responsibility, and to be nurtured by the good word of God ("Strengthening New Members," *LDS Church News*, Nov. 29, 1997).

The worth of souls is great in the eyes of the Lord. The Lord said of His children, that His work and His glory is to bring to pass our immortality and eternal life (see Moses 1:39). Souls are precious, but to gain eternal life they must come into the Church. They must be baptized, but being baptized is not enough. They must endure to the end.

UTILIZING THE BAPTISMAL CHECKLIST

The question is, can we retain these new precious souls? The answer is, yes. We must be as anxious to retain as we are to baptize. The baptismal checklist should be used with utmost accuracy, in every phase of the work. If you follow it—making sure your converts have met the bishop and ward leaders, have had all their interviews and discussions, have set up goals for the temple etc.—the chances of retention are much higher. As missionaries, you should follow up to make sure that everything on the checklist has been taken care of. That the new convert has an opportunity to receive a calling, and if they are men, an opportunity to receive the priesthood. You should do everything in your power, when a person comes into the Church, to help them remain active. So number one, utilize the baptismal checklist both before and after baptism.

CONTINUALLY VISIT

What's the second thing in helping converts remain active? To always make continual visits. People often say, "I don't care how much you know, until I know how much you care." Do you really care about your new converts? Do you really want them to stay active, or do you just want to baptize them so you can have five baptisms for the month, so you can get the award? We baptize people so they can come unto Christ. Our duty as missionaries is to help them press forward with steadfastness; this is why we make continual visits. Remember, when we're making visits to the people, it is important that we live D&C 108:7; the Lord said, "Therefore, strengthen your brethren in all your conversation, in all your prayers, in all your exhortations, and in all your doings." In other words, elders and sisters, at every moment as we open our mouths—in our conversation, as we say our prayers, as we exhort them to come back, in all of our doings—we're doing everything we can to help them return to the Lord. Make sure you enter their names in the area control book. Carefully follow the baptismal checklist. Visits with members are even better. Make sure, when possible, to take a member with you.

THE SIX NEW-MEMBER DISCUSSIONS

Number three: make sure the new converts have the six new-member discussions, because you want them to be nurtured by the word of God and the Spirit. Sometimes you must initiate those. Sometimes you go with the stake missionaries, or sometimes you go with the home teachers. We read in Moroni 6:1–4, that once they've been baptized and entered into the Church and kingdom, their names are kept that they might be continually nourished with the good word of God. Those six new-member discussions are essential. Home teaching and visiting teaching visits are a must. Going to Gospel Essentials classes is crucial. Every chance you have, you want to make sure that these people are nurtured. People can only be nurtured by the Spirit of the Lord, by the power of the word, by faithful, obedient missionaries and members praying with all their heart, might, mind, and soul. Many of your new converts will be lonely, they'll be hurting. You must do everything to make them feel comfortable and at ease in the Church and kingdom of God.

RECLAIMING LESS-ACTIVES

We work with new converts and we also work with the less active—those who have strayed, people who have not made the best choices. I have found that in the Church and kingdom of God, whenever a person goes astray, they have been tempted and have succumbed. They were in a state where these things could happen; where pride, or greed, or lust, or selfishness, or jealousy, or apathy, or ignorance, or even the precepts of men, or the fear of men, or unbelief and vanity, or hypocrisy, or anger became part of their life, and they became less active. Another reason people become less active is because they feel a lack of love—no one cares. The psalmist wrote in Psalms 142:4, "I looked on my right hand, and beheld, but there was no man that would know me: refuge failed me; no man cared for my soul." Feeling unloved is a major cause of inactivity in the Church.

Personal Paths of Righteousness

It's important when working with the less active, that we get them on the path of righteousness, the path to eternal life, the strait and narrow path. Privately, people must begin to do two things—pray and search the scriptures.

In your introduction to the missionary discussions booklet, you'll find the first thing discussed is teaching your investigators how to pray, and committing them to pray.

The Lord said, "Verily, verily I say unto you, ye must watch and pray always, lest ye be tempted." And later on He said, "Verily, verily I say unto you," (pray lest ye be tempted) "for Satan desireth to . . . sift you as wheat" (3 Ne. 18:15,18). Even in our own individual lives, if we don't pray, and if we don't search the scriptures, we'll be tempted and then we'll be less active in some part of the gospel. We may attend our meetings, but we'll be less active in being Saints of the Lord Jesus Christ. These two things are absolutely imperative to being strong in the gospel.

The second topic in the missionary discussion booklet is how to invite people to read and study and ponder the Book of Mormon. A person who is less active must be diligent in searching the scriptures so temptation will not lead them astray.

Laman and Lemuel asked Nephi, "What meaneth the rod of iron?" Nephi responded, "The [rod of iron is the] word of God" (see 1 Ne. 15:24). The only way you can get to the tree of life is by holding to the rod. That's the word of the Lord. There is no other way. And when temptations come over us—the mists of darkness— there's only one way through, and that is by holding to the rod. We live by every word that proceedeth forth from the mouth of the Lord (see D&C 84:43–46); for the words of Christ will tell us all things that we should do (see 2 Ne. 32:3). We learn that the word is indeed a key to avoiding temptation.

For each individual soul—missionary, mother or father, or the teenagers at home—we must search the scriptures, we must fast and pray in order that we not be tempted beyond that which we can endure. That is the way you get other people on the strait and narrow path too.

Fellowship in the Community of Saints

Now that they are on the path that is part and parcel of righteous behavior, the second part is equally important. When people know you care, then they are willing to change. I would write the new English converts and ask them to tell me about their conversion. They would say, "The reason I was converted, President Pinegar, was this: I felt the love of the missionaries so much, I had to listen to what they said. While listening I felt the Spirit and I knew I just had to be baptized." You see, love is important and must be felt.

The third step in activation is the sociality, the fellowship, the coming to church, the going to meetings, so people will tell them how nice it is to see them. And when they start doing that, their lives will change because they feel like part of the kingdom. You might call it a community of the Saints. When you feel that community, you want to be involved with that community.

The other day I was ready to teach my institute class and I looked at one girl whose close friend hadn't arrived yet. And I said, "Hi! How are you doing today?"

"Oh good Brother Ed. I'm great." Her name was Alicia. She was sitting there, and pretty soon her friend Angela walked in the door. Angela caught Alicia's eye, she came in and sat down "Hi!" They smiled as they greeted one another, and they were just so happy together. They just thought it was so great to be together. And I thought, *They come to this class to learn, but they also come because of the sociality and love they feel.* Never, ever let a person feel unnoticed or unloved. When you go to your wards and you see the little children going to primary, walk up and say, "Hi there, young man, you're going to be a great missionary." That's going to make him feel good. When you see those young girls, say, "Hi there! You'll look so good dressed in white when you're married in the temple." In other words, let everybody know that you care about them and give them hope and confidence. That's the sociality of the Saints—fellowshipping and loving because we truly, truly care.

Goals in Visiting the Less Active

When we start working with the less active, we have to visit them. There are four basic groups of less actives: lifetime inactive members who often raise their families in inactivity; new converts who have fallen away, usually in their first year as members; active members who slip into transgression, or for some other reason fall away; and youth who fall away due to the philosophies of men and the influence of their peers.

There are some things to remember in our visits to less active people. Gather as much information as you can about the family before the visit. Visit with the bishop, or their former home teachers. Make sure you get only the information that's proper and reasonably possible. Let the home teacher know about your plan to visit. Remember that in the Church, the missionaries are to visit the less active as part of their member work in missionary service. This is part of being a full-time minister for the Lord Jesus Christ.

Some valuable information to gather might be: (1) Are they a part-member family? (2) What's their marital status? (3) When were they baptized? (4) When was the last time they came to Church? (5) When was the last time they had home teachers?

These kinds of things are valuable to know. Then, before your first visit, pray for the Spirit of the Lord to tell you all things you need to do before you go. Remember, the Lord will prepare a way.

Your first visit should always be short and effective. Be sincere, and show love and concern for the people. Introduce yourselves, tell them you'd like to speak with them. Ask if this is a convenient time— if not, you'll return. Tell them a little about yourself. Ask them about the missionaries who taught them. There's something that happens when that occurs. When converts recall the missionaries who taught them, they become very tender and very sensitive to the Spirit.

For example, I remember once that I sent an elder to High Wycombe for his first area. He arrived in England and the missionaries were making less-active visits. He was taught these very things—to ask less actives about the missionary who taught them. Well, Elder Kennard did, and the man answered, "Oh, she was a wonderful lady. Her name was Sister Loretta Johnson."

Well, Elder Kennard paled, and then he blurted out, "That's my mother. My mother taught you." They were so excited they could hardly stand it, to think that here he was called on a mission, his first area was High Wycombe, and the first week he goes to make the less-active visits, and who does he visit? His mother's less-active convert. Needless to say, the fire was rekindled. Brother Eastley, the inactive member, came back to the Church. Not only that, but his wife, who was not a member, joined the Church as well. Those feelings converts have about their missionaries are always special in their hearts. The Lord knows that, and He certainly works in marvelous ways.

Be sure you express sincere interest in their feelings and their concerns, and discuss their real anxieties. You should be sweetly bold in order to get their concerns out in the open, but most of all, use love and tenderness so as to better understand their true concerns.

In every visit be sure you encourage them to make and keep at least one commitment. Whether it's just the commitment for a return visit, or a commitment to read the Book of Mormon, or a commitment to say their prayers, it is important that a return appointment be set up. As you continue to make these visits, make sure you remember that everyone is different and everyone is special. What might be best for one, may not be best for another.

And as you are visiting these less actives, be sure you correlate this with the ward council, and especially the ward mission leader. When you have a little boy who hasn't been baptized make sure you talk to the Primary president. Or if you have a young beautiful Mia Maid who's about fourteen years old, make sure the Young Women's presidency and the Mia Maid class can visit her. Make sure you correlate your work so everyone in the ward is involved to bless their lives. This is absolutely essential. Continued visits are important in helping them feel the Spirit and in helping them make and keep their commitments.

CONCLUSION

Here are some things to think about when working with hesitant less-actives. (1) Remember that their souls are precious; they must know that you really care. (2) Do you really know how they feel and what they are thinking? Have you asked enough find-out questions? For example: "How did you feel when you attended church? How did you feel when you read the Book of Mormon? Will you come with us to visit Sister So and So?"

All of a sudden, some unrealized concerns may surface. But, you must understand, you'll never know their real condition until you've asked enough questions to know how they really feel and what they are really thinking. (3) Have you used the Book of Mormon as a tool? Is there something in the Book of Mormon that can strengthen them? (4) Have they felt the Spirit and are they aware of it? You must help them identify it and recognize it in their lives. (5) Invite them to make a commitment.

We must feel like Alma. Alma said, as they were going to visit the Zoramites who had gone astray:

> Oh Lord, wilt thou grant unto us that we may have success in bringing them again unto thee in Christ. Behold, O Lord, their souls are precious, and many of them are our brethren; therefore, give unto us, O Lord, power and wisdom that we may bring these, our brethren, again unto thee (Alma 31:34–35).

Now, after our inactive brothers and sisters have felt that Spirit, and they've been made aware of it, you help them resolve their concerns and make and keep their commitments. Make sure that you invite them properly, so that they'll have the power, the staying power, to keep the commitments that the Lord would have them keep. Arrange for a follow-up to help them.

May we remember our duty, not just to baptize, but to retain and keep active all those children of our Heavenly Father by helping them feel the Spirit, and helping them make and keep commitments.

— CHAPTER 14 —

THE MISSION AFTER YOUR MISSION

Elders and sisters return from their missions with much joy and satisfaction. Words from the pulpit sound like, "It was the best two years," or "It was the greatest two years," or "It was the happiest time of my life." Why do missionaries say those words?

WHY THE BEST TWO YEARS?

It's because they are devoted to the Lord; they have spent all their time and all their effort in His behalf, blessing people. They are happy because they spent their lives in building up the kingdom of God. And this means they are helping people come unto Christ. On missions, we all work hard. We're busy. We have a regular schedule. We're always thinking of others and praying for others and pleading with the Lord that they'll come unto Christ.

Sometimes there are days that are frustrating because people are not hospitable. Sometimes we feel persecuted. Sometimes people don't make the commitments. Often times you don't have enough money and you are off your budget. But we don't pursue worldly things. We don't seek after cars, or clothes, or notoriety or fame, or worry about who's winning the game, but just "Who can I bless today?" Every morning we wake up, we search the scriptures for an hour alone and then for another hour with our companion. Then we pray morning, noon, and night. We pray for our investigators, we pray for our companions, we pray for the whole world that they might be happy. We pray to do the Father's will and build up His kingdom. Our lives are focused. We set goals and we make plans: "How many people can we find today? How many are we going to invite to church? How many copies of the Book of Mormon can we place?" This results in preparing people to come unto Christ, and makes our lives focused on one thing, and that is the Lord Jesus Christ and His kingdom.

As we attempt to do this, we are nurtured by the Spirit. We are led by the Spirit. We teach and testify by the Spirit. We enjoy all the blessings of the Spirit from choosing to do good, to do justly, to walk humbly, to judge righteously, to enlighten our minds, to fill our souls with joy, to give us love, peace, long suffering, gentleness, goodness, faith, meekness, and temperance. As missionaries we can enjoy these feelings of the Spirit's companionship. That's why we feel so good building up His kingdom—serving our fellowmen, and the Lord, every moment of our lives.

Why do we do this? Because of the Atonement of Jesus Christ. Christ died so that we might live. For the whole world, for all mankind, He suffered and died that we might return to the presence of our Heavenly Father. And that is why we serve. So, we are saviors on Mount Zion. The Lord said we are the "light unto the world, and to be the saviors of men" (D&C 103:9). We recognize the worth of souls. The Lord said, "How great shall be your joy over a soul that repenteth." And how much greater will it be if many souls repent. And in particular the Lord says how happy He is, and how much joy He has over a soul that repents (see D&C 18:10, 13–16). If we achieve our goals, we have the joy and the fruit of our labors.

I'll never forget the time when two elders were struggling. It was 10:30 at night and the phone rang. Now the missionaries are supposed to be asleep at 10:30, but on the other end of the phone I heard this weeping voice. And I said, "Elder are you OK?"

He said, "Yes, I think so."

I said, "Is your companion OK?"

"Yes, he's OK."

So then I asked, "What's the matter?"

"Sally is not going to be baptized; I just can't stand it."

I said, "Oh Elder, I'm sorry, but she'll be OK."

And then all of a sudden the Spirit came to me and said, "She'll be OK, she'll be baptized."

I said, "Give me her phone number." And so the next morning at 8:30 I called her up and I said, "Sally how do you feel about being baptized?"

She said, "Oh I'm so nervous President Pinegar, I just don't know."

I said, "Well, how do you feel about the Book of Mormon when you read it?"

"Oh I love the Book of Mormon, it's just so good. I want to be good when I read it."

"Well how do you feel about the Prophet Joseph Smith?"

"Oh, he's a prophet."

I said. "That is so good. Have you had a chance to attend church?"

"Oh yes, I've been to church; it's so nice."

I said, "You know what? Since you know this, and you feel this, that's the Spirit telling you that it's true. It's important to follow Christ and keep His commandments and take His name upon you. You know, I was looking forward to coming to your baptism on Sunday night."

"You were?"

I said, "Yes."

Then she said, "Well, OK, I'll be baptized, but I told the elders last night I wouldn't be baptized."

I said, "Don't worry, I'll call them and let them know and they'll call you right back." So I called the elders. I said, "Hello, Elders, it's President Pinegar. Everything's OK, Sally will be baptized."

"Sally will be baptized?" they asked.

I said, "Yes."

Then I promised I'd be there. Well, as I drove up to the Croyden Chapel, one elder was on the outside stairs waiting for us. It was as if they were the brand-new parents of a perfect child. We walked in and the elders said, "President and Sister Pinegar, this is Sally; this is our convert." You would think she was the queen of the world. The worth of souls is great. So when you're a missionary, your mind is thinking only of blessing other people. When you achieve your goals and you have the fruit of your labors, bringing souls unto Christ, you are consumed with the Spirit. You have an overwhelming desire to do good.

On your mission you continually receive support and praise for all that you are doing: letters from parents and friends, the support of the bishopric; your mission president always praising and thanking you for building up the kingdom; confirmation from the Spirit of the great things that you're doing; letters of praise and support and gratitude from converts; and above all, you feel the love of God, knowing that you're on the errand of the Lord Jesus Christ. And these wholesome relationships and feelings you have aren't built upon lust, or greed, or power, or vanity, they're built on your desire to help someone. Yes, as a missionary you have the vision of the work of the Lord, to bring to pass the immortality and eternal life of men. You are always applying correct principles to your life. That's what happens on a mission.

MAINTAINING THE VISION

But when you return home from your mission, things are different—things are really different. There are young men and young women, and you don't have to be one full arm length away, you can actually hold their hands. You can even ask them out on a date, and you would never dare do that on the mission, because that wouldn't be good. Yes, when you return home things really are different. Many people have changed; your little brother's driving your car. He even used your bedroom, and it's still his. You're not quite as organized when you get back. You feel like you're home, you've done your work, you did your mission, it's over—your mission is over. And that is a BIG mistake. Missions are for life. And, guess what else? There's not near as much praise and appreciation. We become kind of self-serving, like, "I've got to do this, and I've got to do that, and I've got to do this, and I need to go over there . . . ." and all of a sudden, it's me, me, me rather than looking out for others. Some days we feel unfulfilled. We rarely make goals and plans to achieve. Our lives become a little undisciplined. We don't recognize the Spirit as much as we did before, for we're not seeking to bless, but rather just to get things done. Sometimes we seem lost because we're not receiving the blessings that we received in the mission field. No regular interviews with the mission president to ask, "How are you doing my son? I love you." Socializing becomes kind of anxious because we don't know how to ask, "Hi would you like to come and go to church with me?" or "Would you like to go on a date?" or "Will you please hold my hand?" I mean, how do you do these things?

The vision of life sometimes becomes obscured, and it's difficult to balance your life, and above all, you miss feeling the Spirit. Now, you're very anxious to get back in the flow of life. Temptations are prevalent, and sometimes because we say to ourselves, "I've worked so hard for two years, or eighteen months, I need to rest. Hallelujah, I don't have to do scripture study, I don't have to get up at 6 AM or 6:30 anymore." And so we sleep in, and when we sleep in we don't have time to search the scriptures, and we become self-indulgent and idle. And whenever we're idle, we will not be happy, for we're not achieving anything worthwhile. We become pleasure seeking, the "me" syndrome happens: my job, my class, my things. And gradually, instead of reaching out to other people, to bless them and serve them, we turn inward and get out of the habits that we need to do in order to be happy

Returned missionaries want to do what's right, but sometimes we don't remember the things we did that brought us happiness. When I was a bishop a few years ago, an elder had just returned from his mission about five or six months before, and he came in and said, "Bishop Ed, I've got to talk to you right now." He was very big, a big strong football player. He said, "I'm not happy anymore," and he began to cry. "My mission was great, and now I don't know what's going wrong. Life is not good. It's the pits. I just wish I was back there, and yet I want to be here. I'm just, I'm just . . . ." He was frustrated, overwhelmed and almost downright discouraged. And then he blurted out, "And I know why. I'm not doing what the Lord wants me to do. Bishop Ed, every day on my mission I searched the scriptures, I studied with my companion, I prayed with real intent to bless people's lives. Now I don't do anything like that at all." Too many missionaries come home saying "I've got to adjust to a new way of living because I'm going to live differently now," and that is a mistake. Life is our mission. We came on this earth to perform a mission, to live here, to help people be happy, and sometimes, when we're out of the mode of being a full-time proselyting missionary, we forget that we're always a missionary. The young women of the Church stand up and say, "We are daughters of our Heavenly Father, who loves us, and we love Him. We will stand as witnesses of God at all times, and in all things, and in all places as we strive to live the Young Women's values which are . . . " (*Young Women's Theme*). You think about that. Young women between twelve and eighteen have the values and standards to stand as witnesses for God at all times, in all things, and all places. Now, that teaches us a principle. Don't seek to adjust to a new way of life, but rather, make your life as a missionary part and parcel of your future life. In other words, the only way to be happy and adjust well is to continue to live by the Spirit. Your life must be a Spirit-directed life. It's a different time in life, but the same principles are involved.

In the mission field, you wanted to find people to whom you could teach the gospel. Well guess what? Now you get to find an eternal companion. Doesn't that sound kind of exciting? Sure, in other words, you want to find that one who you can take to the temple of our God. And this should be a desire; this should be a goal. This isn't something that will just happen. This is something we must work towards. We must get an education. The Spirit can help us choose, guide and direct us on that which we're best qualified to do. Time moves on, and we get married, and guess what? We'll need the Spirit to raise a family. And then we'll all of a sudden realize, I am a son or daughter of God the eternal Father. I am a disciple of Jesus Christ. My duty and obligation here on the earth is always the same: to help people. Whether as a home teacher, or a visiting teacher, Sunday School teacher, Primary teacher—our job is to help people. Well, the same way to help people you learned in the mission field applies in the family, at work, at play and at school. You find out how people are feeling. You present messages. You help them recognize the Spirit because you have taken the time to build a relationship of trust, so your credibility is strong. You'll follow up and see how they're feeling. You'll resolve any concerns. This way of bringing people to Christ is the methodology for how the Spirit works.

One time when I was a bishop, a young return missionary who had been home for about four or five months, came up and said, "Bishop Ed, I've got this new home teaching assignment. I'm going to be seeing Bill and I don't know what to do to help him." Now mind you, he had just returned from a mission. He knows how to help people come unto Christ. But you see what happens—as missionaries, we often compartmentalize the things we learned in the mission field and come home and try to be a new person, and that is the mistake in the adjustment.

I said to him, "Do you know him very well?"

"No not really."

"Well you know, maybe the first thing you ought to do is get acquainted so you can build a relationship of trust and love. You mentioned he doesn't come to church. Well, after you kind of get to know him and find out what he likes to do, you could take him fishing or go skiing or whatever he likes to do. Build on common interests and become better acquainted. Your credibility will be there, and you could present him a little message about coming to church, or going on a double date, or doing something fun. Then pretty soon you could find out how he feels, and when he feels good, then invite him to come to priesthood with you on Sunday morning. 'I'll pick you up about eight.'"

All of a sudden the elder said, "Wait a minute, Bishop Ed, that's how we helped people make commitments on my mission."

I said, "That's right my son, that's the way to help people."

My sweetheart, Sister Pinegar, wrote an article in the February *Ensign* of 1999 on how parents can use this missionary method of committing to help children become truly converted and remain true to the gospel. Don't set aside the things that you learned in the mission field, but rather implement and integrate them into your life. Just as Frederick J. Williams was asked to do, you must be a disciple to lift up the hands that hang down and strengthen the feeble knees (see D&C 81:5). And when you're converted, you strengthen your brethren. How? In all your conversations, in all your prayers and all your doings, and all your exhortations (see D&C 108:7). Your mind is still the same. You don't change focus just because you are home from your mission; you merely focus on different people. Because once you change focus from the gospel of Jesus Christ in your life, your focus will become blurred and the world will ensnare you. Why? Because you will love the things of the world more than the things of God.

This happened even in Adam's time. When Adam and Eve were cast out of the garden Jehovah taught them the plan of redemption. This is found in Moses 5:11–13. And after they'd been taught they thought it was important to make these things known unto their children, and so they did. Then, in verse 13 (a very sad scripture), Satan came among them saying, "I am also a son of God," and then he said "believe it [the gospel] not." And "they loved Satan more than God," and from that time forth they became "carnal, sensual and devilish." Now Elders and Sisters, whenever you set your mind on things of the world—clothes, labels, titles, championships, or any other thing of the world—you will find the world is merely a representation of the adversary. If you love the things of the world, then you don't love God like you should. And as the scripture says, "they loved Satan [and the world] more than God."

Keep the Commandments

So how do we maintain our focus on Christ and building up the kingdom? The Lord, through the Prophet John in the New Testament, said, "If ye love me, keep my commandments" (John 14:15). This becomes an important solution to being happy in the adjustment from your mission.

As the emphasis changes from a full-time proselyting mission to that of a lifelong mission, one thing should be constant—that we do

Heavenly Father's will. If we don't, and it's not in our plans, then righteousness is not ours and we lose. And what do we lose? We lose happiness. King Benjamin said if we are righteous we'll be happy. And if we continue to press forward in righteousness, we'll enter into a state of never-ending happiness (see Mosiah 2:41).

Goals and Self-Discipline

The phase of life following your full-time mission should merely be an extension of your growth, not a separate, compartmentalized time of life. Never compartmentalize the gospel of Jesus Christ. How do we avoid doing this? The solution is clear. We have the Spirit, but we must organize every needful thing. We must have the vision of what we want to accomplish. In the mission field you planned every day: who to visit, who to see, who to bless, and how to help. At home you also need to plan out your day: go to work, visit your home teaching family and the women you visit teach, read your scriptures, pray for your dad, etc. You make a list, a little list of planning to organize every needful time and every needful thing. Your use of time will be better, your educational experience will be better, and your life will be better.

I'll never forget one elder. He'd returned home from his mission and he was going to school, and he wrote me a letter. "Dear President Pinegar, school's going great, everything's good, life is good, life after the mission is terrific. You know what President? You know when you taught us to set goals and make plans? I thought, well that works in the mission field; it ought to work in school. So I took our planner and where it had everything to do with teaching people, I would substitute classes and work and educational experiences and things, and I made my plan to achieve in all those areas. President I just thought you'd want to know that I got a 4.0 this semester, and boy do I feel good." In other words, he was happy because he had achieved, because he had set his goals and made his plans.

Goals are important, and so is the self-discipline we need to accomplish them. In the mission field we had mission rules, and they blessed us and kept us safe. Sometimes when we return home we are so anxious to rid ourselves of the rules that we become totally undisciplined, and we do not have the standards that we once had. Some of the saddest moments I've ever had as a bishop are when missionaries return, and in a few months decide they want to do what they want to do. They sleep in for church, forget to study, don't say their prayers, and they become a little mischievous to say the least. Never let your standards down, because if you do, you will feel guilt. And when that guilt comes upon you, you will be unhappy. So if you let down your standards, you get guilt, you don't feel good, then you lose the Spirit, you feel upset, and you think adjustment life is the pits. And why is it the pits? Because you chose to not be obedient and disciplined.

Most importantly, we must remember that as we make our goals and our plans, we must balance our lives. Intellectual, social, emotional, physical, and above all, spiritual areas are all important. We can balance them so everything has adequate time in relationship to our life.

Prayer and Fasting

There are three major things we must do in order to know every needful thing and stay strong in the kingdom. Too many missionaries return and say, "Oh I've done that." They become casual in their gospel study, casual in their prayers, casual in their attendance at church, casual in their building up the kingdom of God, casual in living a Christlike life, and casual in avoiding and overcoming temptation. Mighty prayer and fasting is absolutely essential to your adjusting as a missionary. The biggest problem is temptation. The Lord said to pray, because Satan wants to sift us as wheat (3 Ne. 18:15, 18). If we're not praying to avoid temptation, we're in trouble. As we learn in Helaman 3:35, we need to pray to increase our humility and faith. We must pray, even as the Nephites prayed, for the desire to have the gift of the Holy Ghost (see 3 Ne. 19:9). For the gift of the Holy Ghost will tell you not some, not most, but *all* things what you should do. Wouldn't you like to be able to just know at any given moment, all the things that are important in your life to do? (2 Ne. 32:5)

A scripture in Alma explains how easy it is to be eligible for the direction of the Spirit. As we learn in Alma 37:37, we should

"Counsel with the Lord in all thy doings." So when we return from a mission we counsel with the Lord in all our doings, and He will direct us for good. So, adjustment won't be hard if we counsel with the Lord. "Yea, when thou liest down at night lie down unto the Lord, that he may watch over you in your sleep; and when thou risest in the morning let thy heart be full of thanks unto God; and if ye do these things, ye shall be lifted up at the last day" (Alma 37:37). If we counsel with the Lord morning, noon, and night, we'll be in tune with the Spirit enough to be directed just as we were on our missions.

Remember when Nephi went back to get the plates? He said, "And I was led by the Spirit, not knowing beforehand the things which I should do" (1 Ne. 4:6). The Spirit comes to us as we have faith, love, and obedience, and pray with all our heart, might, mind, and soul for this gift. Moroni 7:48 says pray with all the energy of your heart that you might be filled with this charity. Remember the love of God? The fruit of the tree which is desirable above all other things to make one happy (see 1 Ne. 8:10)? Well, those who partake of this fruit are happy because they've come unto Christ and partaken of the love of God. That's the difference, you see. When we come to the tree of life and partake of that love, we're happy. You're happy on your mission. Well, you should be doing the same thing at home in order to achieve that same kind of happiness. We start to become like Christ. We receive direction in our life. Our faith and humility become firm and strong. We overcome and avoid temptation. We help others come unto Christ. We help those who are straying. We become righteous. We become happy, and life is sweet if we pray with real intent, having faith in God. If our prayers are casual, so likewise will our life be casual—not focused on the kingdom of God.

Search the Scriptures

The next thing that will ensure we maintain the vision is to search the scriptures. Remember that elder? "I wasn't saying my prayers and I wasn't searching the scriptures." The scriptures will tell us all things that we should do (see 2 Ne. 32:3). We're cautioned, or implored, to live by every word that proceedeth forth from the mouth of God.

When we hold to the iron rod, the mists of darkness, or temptation, will not get us, but we'll be able to press forward and partake of the tree of life. Yes, the word of God has power. It has a greater power to cause men to do that which is just more than anything else (Alma 31:5). That's how powerful the word is. How can we throw away such power, and after only, say, six months, revert back to a previous lifestyle of not searching the scriptures and expect not to feel bad?

Remember what you do with your investigators so they will change? Keep them reading the scriptures, keep them praying, keep them coming to church, keep them trying to do what's right, keep them blessing someone else. The same formula works for me and you. The only way we can stay on the strait and narrow path is by making and keeping commitments. We must always remember what is taught in Helaman 12:2–3, that due to the ease of the way and the comfort which the people enjoyed, guess what happened? They forgot God. When you come home from your mission, and if things become too easy and comfortable, you will find that you will forget; hence, the blessings of happiness are not yours, and adjustment becomes hard. Always remember, as we go to sacrament meeting and partake of the sacrament, we covenant to take His name upon us, remember to keep His commandments. As we remember, then we will be happy because our lives will be focused on our Savior Jesus Christ, and we shall have His Spirit to be with us.

Continue Serving

You can't coast after your mission and live on your life of past service. To feel the Spirit of the Lord and feel good, you must continue in your service. How then do you live the gospel all the time, especially when you're not serving a full-time mission as a set-apart missionary?

One way is through the temple. Sometimes, as we return home, we fail to go back and refresh our minds with the temple and temple worship. As you go to the temple, in the Lord's house, you will find peace and you will find happiness, because this too is an important form of service. Going to the temple will also help reinforce your commitment to your covenants, and you will remember 2 Nephi 31:19–21 and endure to the end.

As you find yourself enduring cheerfully back home, remember those still trying to endure to the end of their missions, or your converts who may need some buoying up. Write some of your old companions. Write some of your converts or some of the ward members to help them and strengthen them in all that they do. Service, either to those still in the field, or here at home for those you meet, will help you keep your focus on the Lord instead of yourself.

Not long ago I wasn't feeling so good. I was getting near retirement and I was worried about whether I had enough money to retire. When you get old you start worrying about things like that because there's not going to be a job, and social security is small, and the little retirement I had set aside was making me kind of nervous. I was thinking about it all the time. I was obsessed with having enough money to live on. I became unhappy because I'd lost my focus. Besides that, the stock market had gone down horribly to the point where I had lost a fair amount of money. Well, I prayed and focused on what to do. With prayer the answer came. "Ed, teach your missionary preparation class with every fiber of your being, bless people's lives." Within almost minutes, because my attitude had changed, I began to feel good again and I was happy. I smiled and I was full of more joy because I wasn't thinking about me and my problem, but rather, "Who can I bless? How can I help?"

As we do all things with the Lord, it's important to remember to be friendly, to look to those we can bless in our families. Sometimes when we come home, when things have changed so much, we feel like no one understands how we feel. And yet, if we're in the mode of service to our family, we'll be surprised at how happy and healthy we will be. And remember this: every day is a test. Every day is a test to prove ourselves worthy to return to the presence of the Lord. Every day, prepare to meet God.

But change is still hard. We go from living a life of total consecration to the Lord and building up the kingdom, to coming back, and the question that haunts us is, "What am I going to do?" When we miss the mission field, we miss the work, companions, the security, the routine, and the mantle that the Lord gave unto us as disciples. As we leave the field, we sometimes leave behind our missionary selves— and that is the mistake. We should still open our mouths. We should still befriend others, always remembering that every good deed we ever do will last forever.

You're Still a Member Missionary

Every moment is a missionary moment. We do not compartmentalize living a Christlike life. We set goals in many areas of our lives that are compatible to bless mankind and build up the kingdom of God, and in doing so we get closer to our Heavenly Father.

Continually building up the kingdom of God requires desire, positive attitude, and work ethic—just like on our missions. It must become our walk and talk. We may all do it differently according to our situations and personalities; but we must eventually open our mouths in order that people might be led to the Lord Jesus Christ.

We can't assume that because we've had the extra opportunity and privilege to serve full-time missions, that we've done our part and now it's up to everybody else. There's a little story about that called "Teamwork," and it goes as follows:

> There were four people named Everybody, Somebody, Anybody, and Nobody. There was an important job to be done and Everybody was asked to do it. Everybody was sure Somebody would do it. Anybody could have done it, but Nobody did it. Somebody got angry about that, because it was Everybody's job. Everybody thought Anybody could have done it, but Nobody realized that Everybody wouldn't do it. It ended up that Everybody blamed Somebody when Nobody did what Anybody could have done.

This bit of humor points out a problem we have in the Church today. Everybody prays that their nice neighbors across the street will join the Church, but they're also hoping that somebody else will be the first to cross that endless chasm and strike up a gospel conversation. We must not be afraid to open our mouths.

There are numbers of ways we can preach the gospel back in our now-busy lives, even with all of our other responsibilities. Start with your own family and work out from there. Write your testimony in the front cover of the Book of Mormon and give it to someone—even friends or relatives (gasp!); or have it translated into several languages and send it out to missionaries in the field. Place the Book of Mormon in your local library. Fellowship people at work, strike up conversations on your way somewhere, or in lines at the grocery store. Fellowship new converts—attend their baptisms and welcome them with open arms. Remember, life goes on after a "no." It's not the end of the world. Just keep loving them, serving them, and keep building up the kingdom.

CONCLUSION

How do we adjust to a whole new way of life? We don't. Life hasn't changed, we're just enduring to the end of our mortal lives instead of to the end of our missions. As you adjusted in the mission field, you'll now need to make that small adjustment as you return. You'll need to build some more relationships of trust. Remember this—time is your ally. Do not be overwhelmed because of the situation and pressures of the day. Don't be impatient. Remember how the Liahona worked? Remember how you plant the seed, and nurture the seed with faith, diligence and patience? So likewise, your patience will be tested as you return home. Allow yourself time to recognize that you will be serving a different kind of mission. The mission of life. Building up the kingdom of God is still a priority, but with family and friends, and at school and work. Now we simply broaden our focus a little. Our lives are still dedicated to the threefold mission of the Church—to perfect the Saints, redeem the dead, and proclaim the gospel.

I want you to remember, with care, the things you learned on your mission and apply them to your mission in life. As you start to date, remember the decency and the patience and kindness and

respect that you learned as a missionary. Treat your date like an investigator. Remember how you were so tender, so loving, and so
thoughtful with your investigators because you cared, and you wanted
them to hear the gospel? Well don't become commanding and
demanding just because you're home. You should treat everyone like
an investigator. Why do we treat investigators so nicely? Because we
want them to come into the kingdom. Well you know what? If we
treat everybody that way, life would be more sweet in all that we do,
and we would all help each other come into the kingdom.

Remember to stay focused on living the gospel every day. Rely on
the Lord, just like you relied on Him before. Be patient in all things
and be sure that your expectation of others is not so high that you
cannot make life fun and happy. Above all, stay busy. Never, ever
lower your standards. Guilt and sin will bring great sorrow.

You might say to yourself, "Well, I know those things." That's
right, you do know everything you have read, but the difference is,
will you remember and apply these things and apply them to your
life? Life will be sweet if you continue on your course of coming unto
Christ, accepting and respecting His atoning sacrifice, and being
perfected by Him in all that you do.

I'd like to end by paraphrasing a little story that will help us
remember the importance of lifelong missionary work; the need to
continually look after our brothers and sisters and lead them into the
fold—to share the precious gift of truth we've been given. It was told
by Dr. Frank Crane, and it's called "The Shoeless Town."

One day a man had occasion to visit another town on business.
He arrived at the station on a cold December day. As he walked along
he saw women dressed in costly furs, gentlemen in fur coats and fancy
suits. All of them were adorned with diamonds and pearls and expen-
sive packages. The strange thing about the scene, was that everyone
was barefoot. In spite of their great wealth, they limped along, and
were afflicted with bruises and cuts, and they suffered great pain.

When he went to the hotel he found more of the same—all the bell-
boys and other attendants also went barefoot. In fact, no one in the town
wore shoes. At the dinner table he met an old, distinguished-looking

gentleman and fell into conversation with him. The old man seemed kind and open-minded, so the stranger asked about the bare feet in the dead of winter. "Ah!" said the old gentleman, raising his eyes piously, "Why indeed!" Which response did not answer the businessman's question. He couldn't get a straight answer from the man. He even agreed that shoes were most desirable above all other things—especially in December—but couldn't explain why no one bothered to wear them.

As the man left the restaurant, he passed a shoe factory. He asked a nearby janitor if the factory produced the town's shoes; and if it were perhaps in a state of disrepair. But the good-natured janitor simply responded, "Oh, not at all. They just talk about making shoes, and sing songs about shoes, and pray about them."

This answer perplexed the stranger. He looked about him for some explanation, and saw only a sign advertising that the chief official of the factory was going to give several upcoming lectures on shoes: the origin of shoes, the history of shoemaking, the varieties of leather, etc. Now, almost annoyed, the man loudly questioned the wisdom in this. But no one paid any heed.

Just before reaching his hotel, he passed by a small shop in which an old German cobbler was making a pair of shoes. Excited, he purchased the pair and took them to the kindly old gentleman he had dined with. To his surprise, the man declined the gift, assuring the bewildered giver that none of the best people ever wore shoes. That it was considered a sign of fanaticism.

Dr. Crane sums up the moral of the story; noting that it's a pity that the most usable force in the world for developing character, bringing people closer to God, and making happiness—religion—should be so shameful to us that we are afraid to claim that we have it and use it.

I would sum it up in one sentence: "Truth without testimony is hollow." We must live it and bear it. Like the Apostle Paul, we must declare that we "are not ashamed of the gospel of Christ"—that we are willing to put on the whole armor of God, including the "shoes" of the gospel (see Rom. 1:16; Eph. 6:13–17). And thus being shod, may we be willing to share with our brothers and sisters the happiness it can bring.

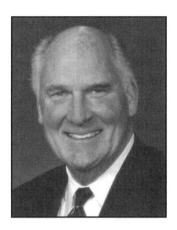

ABOUT THE AUTHOR

Ed J. Pinegar graduated from Brigham Young University in 1956 with a degree in chemistry and mathematics. He attended dental school at the University of Southern California, during which time he taught early morning seminary.

Upon returning to Provo to begin his dental practice, he again taught early morning seminary and Book of Mormon and Gospel Principles and Practices classes at BYU. Brother Pinegar presently serves part time on the faculty at the Orem Institute of Religion at Utah Valley State College in Orem, Utah, and is a teacher at the Senior MTC in Provo.

Some of Brother Pinegar's former Church callings include: President of the England, London South Mission; President of the Missionary Training Center in Provo, Utah; and member of the Missionary Programs Advisory Committee.

Brother Pinegar has produced numerous talk tapes, including several volumes of *Especially for Missionaries*. He has taught many Continuing Education programs and was a recipient of the Excellence in Teaching Award in 1979.

Brother Pinegar is married to Patricia Peterson Pinegar, who formerly served as General President of the Primary for the Church, and they are the parents of eight children, thirty grandchildren, and one great-grandchild.

the
MISSIONARY'S
LITTLE BOOK
of
Inspirational
Stories

As a Man Thinketh . . .

A wise man stood at the gate of an ancient city and greeted travelers as they arrived. One day, a traveler asked him:

"What kind of people live in this city?"

The wise man responded with a question of his own: "What kind of people lived in the city from whence you came?"

"Oh, they were very bad people," answered the traveler, "cruel, deceitful, and devil-worshipping."

"You'll find the same kind of people in this city," sighed the wise man.

Some time later, a second traveler came to the gate and asked about the people in the city. The wise man again asked his question:

"What kind of people lived in the city from whence you came?"

"Oh, they were very good people," answered the second traveler, "hard-working, generous, and God-fearing."

"You'll find the same kind of people in this city," smiled the wise man.

– AS TOLD BY KIMBERLY EVANS JONES

Word of Honor

"My friends, I have been asked what is meant by 'word of honor.' I will tell you. Place me behind prison walls—high, thick walls of stone. It is possible that somehow I could escape. But stand me on the floor, draw a chalk line around me and have me give my word of honor not to cross it and I would never cross the line. I'd die first!"

– Karl G. Maeser

Self-Possession

I walked with my friend to the newsstand the other night. He bought a paper and thanked the newsie politely. The newsie didn't even acknowledge him.

"A sullen fellow, isn't he?" I commented.

"Oh, he's that way every night," shrugged my friend.

"Then why do you continue to be so polite to him?" I asked.

"Why not?" inquired my friend. "Why should I let him decide how I'm going to act?"

As I thought about this incident, it occurred to me that the important word my friend used was "act." My friend acts, while most of us react to people. He has a sense of inner balance most of us lack. He knows who he is, what he stands for, and how he should behave. He refuses to return incivility for incivility, because he controls his own conduct.

We must become masters of our own actions and attitudes. To let another person determine whether we will be rude or gracious, elated or depressed, is to give up control of ourselves. The only true possession is self-possession.

– Sydney J. Harris

Two Buckets

Two buckets were sitting on the edge of a well. One turned to the other with mouth drooping down, "All I do is go down and come up and go down and come up all day long. No matter how many times I come up full, I always go down empty."

The other bucket gave a warm smile." That's funny," she said." I do the same thing. All I do is go down and come up and go down and come up all day long. But no matter how many times I go down empty, I always come up full."

– Bits and Pieces

Look to This Day!

Look to this day!
For it is life, the very life of life.
In its brief course lie all the varieties and realities of your existence:
The bliss of growth;
The glory of action;
The splendor of beauty;
For yesterday is already a dream, and tomorrow is only a vision;
But today, well lived, makes every yesterday
A dream of happiness, and every tomorrow a vision of hope.
Look well, therefore, to this day.
– FROM THE SANSKRIT

A Tale of Two Frogs

Two frogs fell into a deep milk bowl.
One of them had an optimist's soul,
While the other took a gloomier view:
"We shall drown," he cried, without further adieu,
And with one last despairing cry,
He flung up his legs and said goodbye.

Said the other frog with a merry grin,
"I can't get out, but I won't give in;
I'll keep swimming around till my strength is spent,
Then at least I'll die the more content."

So bravely he swam, until it would seem,
His struggles began to churn the cream.
And on top of the butter at last, he stopped—
then out of the bowl he gaily hopped.
What of the moral? It's easily found:
If you cannot hop out, keep swimming around.
– ANTHONY P. CASTLE

The Drug Store

A few months after moving to a small town, a woman complained to a neighbor about the poor service at the local drug store. She hoped the neighbor would repeat her complaint to the store's owner.

The next time she went to the drugstore the druggist greeted her with a big smile and told her how happy he was to see her again. He said he hoped she liked their town and to please let him know if there was anything he could do to help her get settled. He then filled her order promptly and courteously.

Later the woman reported the miraculous change to her friend. "I suppose you told the druggist how poor I thought the service was?" she asked.

"Actually," the woman said. "I told him you were amazed at the way he had built up his drug store and you thought it was one of the best you'd ever seen."

– AUTHOR UNKNOWN

The Man Who Thinks He Can

If you think you are beaten, you are;
If you think you dare not, you don't.
If you like to win, but think you can't;
It's almost a cinch you won't.

If you think you'll lose, your lost.
For out in the world we find,
Success begins with a fellow's will;
It's all in the state of mind.

If you think you are outclassed, you are;
You've got to think high to rise.
You've got to be sure of yourself before
You can ever win the prize.

Life's battles don't always go
To the stronger and faster man;
But sooner or later the man who wins
Is the man who thinks he can.

– WALTER D. WINGLE